Practical Jazz Piano

©Robert Larson 2021
All rights reserved. No part of this book may be used or reproduced by any means, graphic, electronic or mechanical, including photocopying, recording, taping or any information storage or retrieval system without written permission of the author.

With Special Thanks:

As with all of my projects, I am grateful for the support of family, friends, students, and musical colleagues. In particular: Karen, Rachel, Sarah (my family); Cathy Nelson – also family – for her careful editing; Craig Fraedrich, Matt Niess, Tony Nalker, Golder O'Neill, Alan Baylock, Bill Linney, (friends and colleagues, to name a few very important ones); and students (too numerous to name) – I've learned so much from helping you in your musical journeys.

Thank you all.

About the Author

Robert Larson is a jazz pianist, composer, and educator. He served as the Director of Jazz Studies at Shenandoah University in Winchester, Virginia for thirty years and was a member of the faculty for thirty-nine years. He holds degrees from Eastern Washington University, the University of Oregon, and Shenandoah Conservatory. He taught courses in jazz history, jazz improvisation, jazz arranging, jazz and traditional music theory, jazz repertoire, and jazz pedagogy. He conducted the Shenandoah Conservatory Jazz Ensemble from 1987-2000, and during that time the ensemble performed with prominent guest artists, including Randy Brecker, Billy Taylor, Bob Berg, Al Vizzutti, and many others, and toured China, Japan, Spain, France, and Iceland. His book, *Arranging for the Small Jazz Ensemble* (Armfield Academic Press) is used in jazz arranging courses throughout the United States. He has published articles in the *College Music Society Symposium,* the *Music Educators Journal,* the *Virginia Music Educators Association Journal,* and the *International Association of Jazz Educators Papers*. He has presented at jazz education conferences on the early recordings of Bill Evans, critical listening, and arranging techniques. He released his CD *Popular Delusions* in 2016, and it has received extensive nationwide radio play. He can also be heard on recordings with the *Alan Baylock Jazz Orchestra*, the most recent featuring Doc Severinsen. He performs with his own trio, and is an in-demand sideman in the Washington DC region. He has served on the touring panel for the *Virginia Commission for the Arts*, the board of *First Night Winchester*, and was the host of the *National Jazz Workshop* at Shenandoah University from 2008 to 2020.

Contents

Preface i
Some Basics v

Part I: Voicings and Harmonic Progression   1

1 Simple Voicings... 5
      Triads.. 5
      Triad Inversions.. 11
      Sevenths... 11
      Seventh Chord Inversions 16
      Guide Tone Voicings... 17
      Harmonizing a Melody 20

2 Simple Harmonic Progression 23

3 Four-Way Close Voicings, Tonal Clusters, and Chord Tone Substitution 27
      Four-Way Close Voicings.. 27
      Chord Tone Substitution 29
      Tonal Clusters 38

4 Advanced Harmonic Progression: Four-Way Close Voicings 41
      Four-Way Close ii-V-I 41
      Adding a Secondary Dominant, Creating a Turnaround 43
      Close Position Progressions: Going Beyond the Four-Note Structure 50

5 Open Position Voicings.. 53
      Drop-2 53
      Quartal Structures 56
      So What Voicings... 59
      Slash Chords 61
      Open Position Voicings with Tonal Clusters 64

6 Open Position Harmonic Motion 67
      Drop-2 – ii-V-I-V/ii Motion 67
      Quartal, *So What,* and Slash Chords – ii-V-I Motion 68
      GLT I and *II*: Quartal, *So What,* and Slash Chord Comping............ 70

7 Three-Part Voicings.. 73
      Shell Voicings... 73
      Quartal Voicings and Clusters... 73
      Three-Part Chords in a Progression 74
      Three-Part Left Hand Voicings 75

8 Re-Harmonization Principles.. 77
      Functional Re-Harmonization... 77
      Non-Functional Re-Harmonization.. 79

Part II: Rhythm and Style — 81

9 Comping 85
- Swing Comping 85
- Latin Comping 87
- Rock Ballad Comping 89
- Broken Chord Comping 90
- Comping with Large Chords 91
- Funk Comping 92

10 Special Techniques 93
- Bass Lines 93
- Locked Hands 97
- Red Garland Block Chord Method 100
- Stride 102
- Boogie Woogie 103

Part III: The Improvised Line — 107

11 Scales and Melodic Formulae for Individual Harmonies 111
- Major Sevenths - Scales 111
- Major Sevenths – Melodic Formulae 112
- Minor Sevenths – Scales 113
- Minor Sevenths – Melodic Formulae 114
- Half Diminished – Scales 115
- Dominant Sevenths – Dual Roles 116
- Dominant Sevenths – Scales 116
- Resolving and Non-Resolving Dominants – Melodic Formulae 120
- Improvising with Various Rhythmic Values 122

12 Scales and Melodic Formula Over Common Progressions 125
- One Chord Per Four/Four Measure Harmonic Rhythm 126
- Two Chords Per Four/Four Measure Harmonic Rhythm 130
- Improvising with Various Rhythm Values 131

Part IV: Creating a Performance — 133

13 Creating Transitional Material 137
- Choral and Linear Methods 137

14 Introductions 141
Common Introduction Types 141

15 Endings 147
- Common Ending Types 147

16 *Guided Learning Tunes*: Complete Versions 155

Guided Learning Tune I 156
Guided Learning Tune II 163

Appendices   171

Appendix A: Chord/Scale Summary 173

Appendix B: Scale Fingerings 175

Appendix C: Suggested Jazz Theory Books 179

Appendix D: Select Discography 183

Preface

    The piano's position of importance in the history of western classical music is undeniable; the same can be said of the jazz idiom. From the origins of the music, beginning with ragtime and continuing throughout each important stylistic innovation, the piano has played a vital role. The characteristics of the piano – its enormous range, dynamics, power, and harmonic possibilities – have ensured its inclusion in almost all jazz settings. While the solo jazz piano artist has played a significant part in the history of the music, the development of jazz has been one of collaboration and influence. Specifically, the combination of the harmonic and rhythmic underpinnings provided by pianists merged with the evolution of the improvised melodic line epitomized by horn players in group settings. Thus the pianist, as both solo artist and ensemble member, has and will continue to play a vital role in the continuing development of jazz.

    Because of the nature of the instrument, the solo jazz pianist can combine melody, harmony, and a bass voice. Jelly Roll Morton, in his interview with Alan Lomax at the Library of Congress in 1938, states that he always "played like a band" at the piano.[1] The solo pianist can imitate all of the sections of a band, which Morton ably demonstrates, and therefore pianists often have a more 'global' approach to a performance than perhaps other instrumentalists. When combined in an ensemble, however, pianists are much more than mere accompanists. Often the pianist is called upon to improvise a solo introduction; he also will probably play an improvised solo along with the rest of the rhythm section (in essence turning a standard small jazz group into a 'jazz piano trio').

    The breadth of harmonic and textural possibilities available to a jazz pianist also brings with it the challenge of collaboration. A pianist performing within a band shouldn't imitate a band in her own playing, but figure out a way, through careful listening and a sensitivity to the other players, to 'fit in'. The history of jazz piano can be analyzed in this way – of how the pianist 'fits in' to various ensemble settings. The best jazz pianists (i.e., the ones who get the most work) are able to make everyone else sound good.

    This book is meant to provide foundational material for novice pianists, but it also includes some advanced techniques. It should be used alongside a good jazz theory text; while there are theoretic concepts addressed throughout, <u>this is not a jazz theory book</u>. The reader should be able read the grand staff, have a decent technique (preferably gained from classical study), should know major and the three forms of minor scales, arpeggios, and the fundamentals of traditional music theory. Please realize that if you are not familiar with the diatonic and melodic minor mode systems, pentatonic and diminished scales, basic jazz harmonic principles (the ii-V-I progression, tritone substitution, the blues), and common jazz forms, you may need to reference other sources for these concepts. There is a chord/scale summary in Appendix A that will be helpful in answering questions, and will hopefully lead you to more research and inquiry. In addition, Appendix C contains of a list of some of my favorite jazz theory books.

---

[1] Jelly Roll Morton, interviewed by Alan Lomax, *Discourse on Jazz,* The Library of Congress Recordings, Volume 8. (Australia: Swaggie Records, 1938).

How to Practice

There are four kinds of "sensory/brain understandings"[2] that occur simultaneously for pianists: tactile, where we notice and feel shapes with our hands; visual, where we view the keyboard (a real advantage for pianists over other instrumentalists and vocalists); analytical, where we use our theoretical knowledge; and aural, where we hear a sound and understand its role. All of these activities need to be active while we practice.

I have found in over 40 years of teaching jazz piano that students sometimes struggle with the organizational aspect of the learning process in this specialized music, particularly those that have a traditional background. Preparing a classical piece of music is fairly clear cut – the player should practice hands separately, should 'divide and conquer', and practice slowly enough so that mistakes are minimized. Transferring these steps to learning jazz and jazz improvisation is possible, but with some modifications. The issue is that the player will be to a large degree inventing the music as she goes along. This is very different from attempting to perfect a composed piece of music. That being said, much of the process is the same – hands-separate practice, played at a slow pace, and divided into 'chunks' is a highly effective method. By far the most important element is *focused repetition*. It is critical to memorize chord voicings, progressions, melodies, scales, patterns, and theoretical concepts so that the player can create and react quickly to circumstances that arise. To achieve this, you must do the following:

1. Drill and repeat everything you work on in all keys, which means slowly enough so that mistakes are minimized. Music is hard enough the first time – it's much more difficult when something learned incorrectly has to be 'erased' and then learned correctly. Moving through the keys is best achieved by varying the pattern, i.e., circle of fourths, chromatically, in thirds, in whole steps, and even randomly.
2. Apply what you've practiced to jazz standards with careful thought and planning.
3. Use your ears constantly, but make sure that you're not completely relying on hearing to determine if what you're working on is correct – ensure that you *know* it's correct. (I sometimes have students practice on an electric keyboard that is powered off, and therefore with no aural confirmation of correctness or mistakes).
4. Listen and transcribe. Perhaps this seems obvious, but with so much music available to all of us in the digital age, one must prioritize listening; you can't play a style of music if you don't know what it sounds like. There is a discography of some personal favorite recordings in Appendix D.
5. Play with other musicians – not just with play-along recordings. Jazz is a participatory music. Plus, we learn from one another. Form bands, attend jam sessions – get involved with other players as much as possible.
6. Record yourself. A microphone is your best teacher.

---

[2] Phil DeGregg, *Jazz Keyboard Harmony: A Practical Method For All Musicians* (New Albany, IN: Jamey Aebersold Jazz, Inc., 1994), 2.

How this book is organized

This book is meant to be practical. Although there are books on the market that contain many facets of jazz piano playing, this comprehensive book does so in a concise fashion that offers common sense and simple solutions to the art of jazz piano. The heart of this book is divided into four parts that correspond to specific musical elements – harmony; rhythm and style; the improvised line; and 'creating a performance'. The harmony unit is comprised of voicing techniques, harmonic motion, texture, and an overview of re-harmonization. The rhythm and style unit delves into comping, bass lines and some specialized techniques pioneered by the giants of jazz piano. The unit devoted to improvisation focuses on scales and common melodic formulae. The final unit merges the material, adds information about how to construct transitions, introductions, endings, and includes examples of complete performances. While these elements are divided and tackled individually, there naturally is much overlap. It is important to continually reference various sections of the text. Like in my arranging book, *Arranging for the Small Jazz Ensemble* (Armfield Academic Press), instructional tunes, called *Guided Learning Tunes (GLT)* have been composed that will be used throughout to illustrate various concepts. The lead sheets for the two *GLT*s are presented below. Practice these melodies and study the harmonic motion.

Exercises

There are exercises in each chapter to help with the assimilation of the material. Most involve practicing and memorizing voicings, melodic formula, and progressions in all keys. Some, especially those early in the book, are notated in all keys; later, transposition is required by the player – certainly a vital skill for pianists.

Recordings

There are recordings of many of the examples and all of the *Guided Learning Tunes I and II* illustrations. The recordings are performed as solo piano pieces, in a trio setting (piano, bass, and drums) and in a few cases, either as a duo or quartet, with flute taking the melody. Complete versions of the tunes are notated in Chapter 16. The recordings can be found on YouTube under the book title or by using the QR code on the back cover. Look for this icon next to the examples:

Guided Learning Tunes I and II

GLT I resembles the "A" section of the standard *What's New*. This eight measure tune moves from the home key of C major into the borrowed sub-medient key of A♭ – a very colorful tonal shift, through a ii-V-I progression. It also moves into C minor – again with a ii-V motion (note the half-diminished chord built on ii – the diatonic ii chord in minor), and resolves back to C major leading to the turnaround. The harmonic motion of *GLT I* is designed to highlight the differences between the major and minor systems. The style and tempo would indicate a tempo of about mm = 120 in a swing style, but as with most jazz standards, it can be performed in a variety of tempos and styles. The complete version, in Chapter 16, includes a bridge so that it unfolds in a standard AABA form.

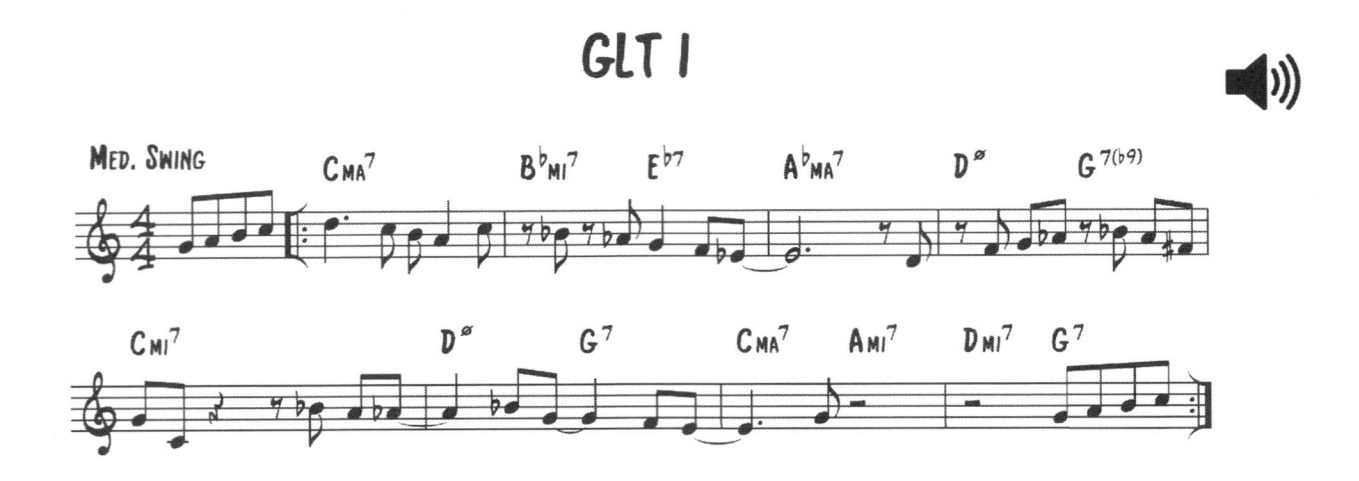

GLT II is a 12-bar blues in F. This simple melody is derived from the major blues scale. Note that this is a blues progression commonly found in the bebop era, with traditional harmonic motion leading to and during the last phrase (the D7-G7-C7-F7 motion is a cycle of dominants). The style is 'swing' with no tempo indication; it could be performed at a variety of tempos, which is true of many blues. The tempo of the complete version in Chapter 16 is mm=150.

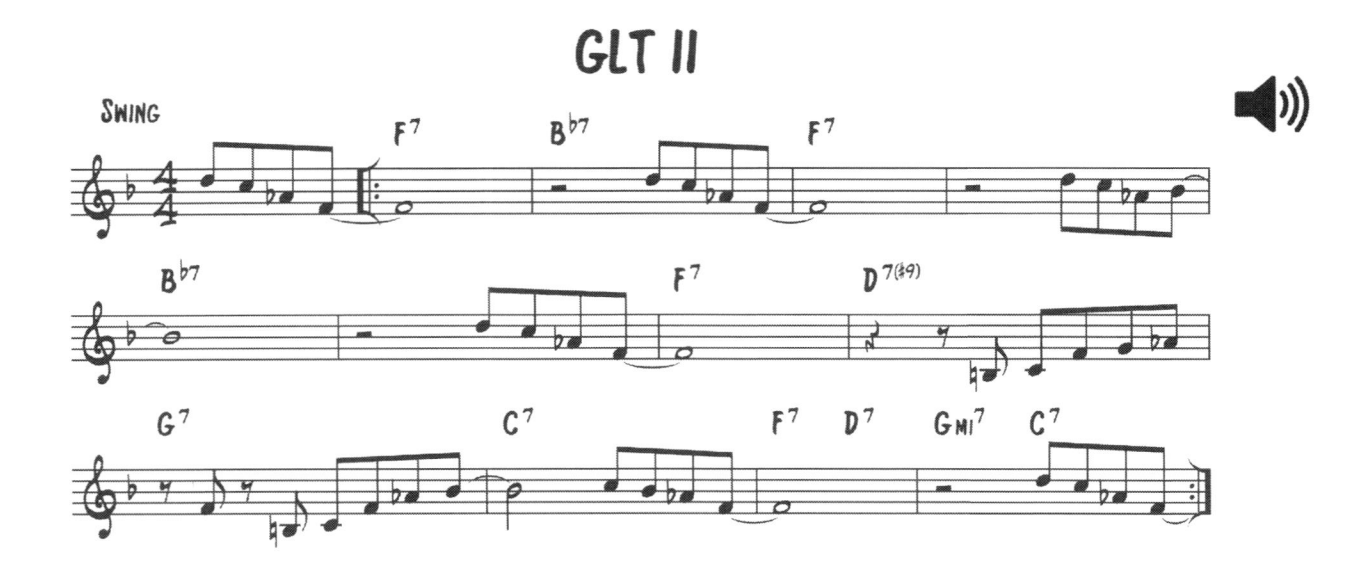

Finally, the book begins with a section on some basic concepts that should be understood thoroughly before moving forward.

Some Basics

Texture

A word often used in the creation of all types of art forms is *texture*. Texture is a broad term describing how something is constructed. In music, texture is formed by combining the melodic, rhythmic, harmonic, and formal elements in a particular way. The resulting creation is also combined with the relationship among volume levels throughout the performance, instrumentation, and tempo. Because of the nature of the piano, with its range, dynamics, power, and harmonic possibilities, pianists govern much of how a piece of music unfolds, and therefore its texture. A fundamental question involving texture is the following: what specifically does each hand do when playing jazz piano? That depends upon the setting (solo, trio, quartet, big band), style of music, and to a large degree, tempo. Think about it like Jelly Roll Morton (referenced above) – when you're playing the piano you're imitating the sound of a band. Ensembles of all types, in all kinds of music, normally have a melody (either composed or improvised), harmony, and usually a bass foundation. Therefore, there are <u>three</u> 'layers' that need to be covered, with our <u>two</u> hands. When playing with a bassist, we obviously have only two layers to cover, so the harmony can be played in the left hand and the melody in the right. In a duo setting with a horn player or singer, we can place the harmony in the right hand, and the left hand can provide the foundation, and can even play the role of a bassist (walking bass lines, Latin bass lines, etc.). The tricky part is when we're playing as soloists, because the three layers must be played by two hands. A common approach is to place the melody on top of the chords in the right hand and play the bass part – often just the chord roots – in the left. This works well when performing jazz standards, most especially the music of the 'Great American Song Book' – tunes like *I Can't Get Started, A Foggy Day, Here's That Rainy Day* and many others. However, in modern styles (that is, bebop and beyond), the texture employed by pianists can be described as *minimalistic*, where players and listeners are comfortable with a 'layer' missing. Often pianists omit the bass voice (but include the striking of a bass note here and there, as heard frequently in Bud Powell's playing), and place rootless voicings in the left hand with the right hand acting as the 'featured soloist'. Older styles, such as *stride* (where the bass and chords are combined into an energetic left hand accompaniment pattern complementing the right hand melody), or *boogie woogie* (where a hard-driving left hand accompaniment, known as 'eight to the bar' is utilized to accompany a bluesy right hand line) while still valid, are not practical as jazz increased in tempo and complexity into the bebop era. However, a versatile jazz pianist should be able to perform in many styles, and examples will be provided in Part II.

Style

Jazz music encompasses a wide range of styles. This becomes evident by simply scanning the table of contents in a jazz history textbook. New Orleans style, swing era, bebop, hard bop, cool, fusion, free jazz – these are categories that make up most of the jazz canon.

While it is important to become versed in all of these styles, pianists should at a minimum be comfortable in *swing* (as in, utilizing the swing eighth note feel and the associated accent patterns), Latin (at least the *bossa nova* style), and *fusion* (the combination of a rock rhythmic feel, of which there are many, with the jazz harmonic language). The style aspect of the music is at least as important as studying jazz harmony and melodic construction, and is accomplished through listening and playing experience.

Fingering Tips

When playing four note chords (a common number of notes in a single hand, as we'll see below), utilizing the thumb, index, middle, and pinky finger for both hands is the most frequent fingering. Major and minor scale fingerings are of course standardized and extremely helpful as a foundation when playing either written melodies or improvising lines. These can be extended to mode fingerings as well, as modes are essentially major scales beginning at various points of a parent scale. A particular challenge is the 'improvisation' of fingering – that is, when we're creating melodies on the spot, we're also by extension creating fingerings. This is why the foundation of standard scale fingerings is so important. There are fingering charts in Appendix B that include traditional and non-traditional scales, such as diminished, pentatonic, and bebop scales.

Range for Chords

Where to place chords on the piano keyboard depends upon several factors. Composers such as Duke Ellington and Charles Mingus were fond of dark sonorities, and were capable of great flexibility in voicing chords. Red Garland's block chord voicings were placed on the upper end of the keyboard to great effect. For the purposes of this book, assume that a chord normally should not be placed below 'D' below middle C. Theoretically, chords can be placed at the extreme upper register, but the resulting timbre will be very thin. The middle of the keyboard is your best choice.

Enharmonic Spellings

Jazz notation is commonly written 'wrong' from a theoretical standpoint. The reason for this is simple – ease of reading. So a word of warning – if you are confused about why a certain note is included in a chord, think about a different spelling and that may clear up your confusion. For example, a chord containing an E natural and an E flat is common within a C chord. The E is a major third and the E flat is not a minor third, but a raised ninth (which should theoretically be notated as a D♯). Get used to it!

Jazz Chord Notation

The notation system used in the jazz idiom offers an extremely efficient method to quickly identify chords. A brief discussion of this unique system is included here because of its importance in the upcoming examination of voicing techniques and options. It is often referred to as 'lead sheet notation'; I prefer the term 'jazz chord notation' as it was originally developed as a vocabulary for jazz musicians. One must understand this system so thoroughly that no thought or hesitation is required as a chord is being read and subsequently played. Fortunately, the simplicity of the system allows for this level of expertise. Think of how easy it is to play a single note on the keyboard; that is how quickly one must be able to play a chord like Dma7♯11. As specific chords are described in the pages that follow, the notation system will be explained. For now, it is important to realize two fundamental principles: 1) the system is independent of the key in which the chords exist, unlike 'figured bass' from traditional theory study, which is governed by the key and, 2) the words major and minor have specific roles that are as follows: "major" refers only to the seventh of a chord; "minor" refers to the third. Finally, you'll want to consult a jazz theory text for information regarding specialized symbols that go beyond the basic system described here. Symbols such as "alt" and using mode names in symbols (such as "F dorian" as a chord symbol) and even the very open-ended symbol "-ish", as in "D-ish" are three examples. Again, consult a jazz theory text for more information. Finally, this book will use "ma" for major and "mi" and "-" for minor; however, there are other symbols that are quite common, including a triangle that denotes major.

The Circle of Fifths/Fourths

The circle of fifths can be illustrated as a circular graph representing the extremely important arrangement of key relationships that must be memorized. You will recall from your theory study that music often moves in falling fifths. On the circle, this would be in a counterclockwise direction – <u>also known as the circle of fourths</u> (i.e., C-F-B♭, etc). This movement is central to all 'common practice' music, and is especially important to jazz musicians, as it dominates the music.

Refer to your jazz theory texts for information about the circle. It will be used as a drill throughout the book. Below is a diagram of this important concept.

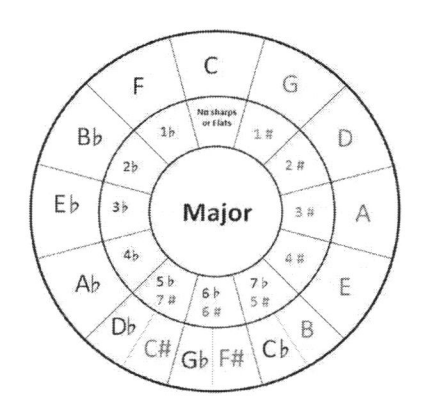

Part I
Voicings and Harmonic Progression

Part I introduces triads, sevenths, upper extensions, chord tone substitution, voicing types, tertian, quartal, and secundal harmony and common chord progressions. Exercises are provided that are to be memorized; chord voicings and progressions must be at the level of an automatic response. The direct thought process of jazz should be at a very high level, where musical and creative decisions are made; to do this, the fundamentals must be deeply ingrained. Use the notated chords as a starting point, but strive to be able to play them from memory as well as by viewing only a chord symbol. The circle of fourths diagram in the preface should be used for this.

1
Simple Voicings

The term "voicing" refers to the distribution of chord tones between the hands, or by an ensemble. A chord can be expressed with as little as two notes (often the third and seventh) or can contain all of the possible tones, including the upper extensions (these will be explained as we move forward). Normally, one type of voicing is used for a given passage, although the player can move among different voicing possibilities depending on the circumstance. Chords are often played without roots (so-called "rootless voicings"), especially in the left hand, or in the right hand when in an accompanying situation. When the pianist is stating the melody, the melodic tones will help determine your choice as well, as the melody is normally the top note of the structure. Chords can be thought of as stacks of thirds, fourths and fifths, and in a 'close position' – within an octave – or in 'open position' – chords that span more than an octave. Tonal clusters (secundal harmony) are also important tools for jazz pianists. Descriptive terms will be explained throughout the book, and exercises are provided. This first chapter focuses on tertian structures, that is, chords built in thirds. Along with presenting these simple structures, lead sheet notation will be explained as well. While the reader may be familiar with this basic material, the discussion of lead sheet notation is necessary in order to understand the process of expanding tertian structures beyond the triad.

Triads

Example 1-1 illustrates a major triad, constructed of a major third and perfect fifth. It is identified by only its letter name, in this case, "C". This is a "tertian" structure, as it is constructed of stacked thirds.

Example 1-1 The Major Triad

Example 1-2 contains a minor triad, constructed of a minor third and perfect fifth. Its symbol requires the word "minor", usually abbreviated to 'min', 'mi', or a dash symbol (C-).

Example 1-2 *The Minor Triad*

The other two types of triads are shown in Example 1-3. The diminished triad contains a minor third and diminished fifth; its symbol is a small circle. The augmented triad contains a major third and an augmented fifth; its symbol is the letter name followed by a "+" sign.

Example 1-3 *The Diminished and Augmented Triads*

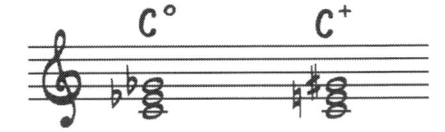

Triad Exercises

As described above, there are four qualities of triads: major, minor, diminished, and augmented. The following exercises contain all of the chords notated, and with chord symbols. Ultimately, all exercises in this book must be memorized. Note that the left hand plays the chord root. These are notated only for the first exercise. Obviously, the chord root can be found by simply reading the chord symbol. Drill these using a metronome to gauge your progress. You MUST reach the point where these are AUTOMATIC. When practicing the chords in the left hand, the right hand should rest (though I have had students who have used the stronger right hand to 'teach' the left hand by playing the chords in two hands, simply doubled at the octave).

Simple Voicings

Exercise 1-1: Major Triads – Circle of Fourths

Practice triads by moving around the circle of fourths. Play the chords in the right hand and the roots in the left; then practice the chords in the left hand while the right hand rests.

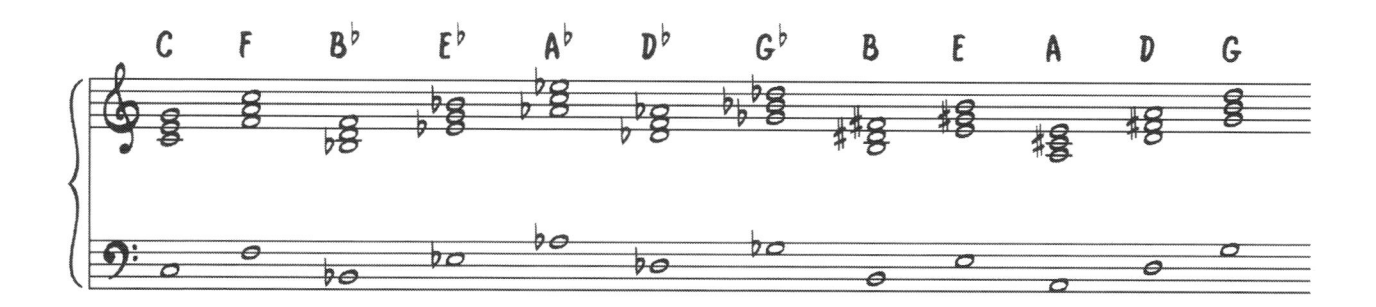

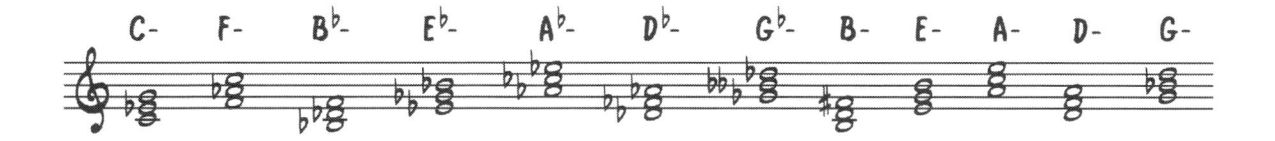

Exercise 1-2: Major Triads - Chromatic

Practice triads chromatically, ascending and descending. Play the chords in the right hand and the roots in the left; then practice the chords in the left hand while the right hand rests.

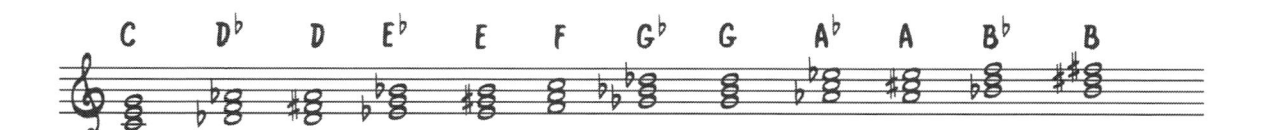

Exercise 1-3: Minor Triads – Circle of Fourths

Practice triads by moving around the circle of fourths. Play the chords in the right hand and the roots in the left; then practice the chords in the left hand while the right hand rests.

8   Part I: Voicings and Harmonic Progression

Exercise 1-4: Minor Triads - Chromatic

Practice triads chromatically, ascending and descending. Play the chords in the right hand and the roots in the left; then practice the chords in the left hand while the right hand rests.

Exercise 1-5: Diminished Triads – Circle of Fourths

Practice triads by moving around the circle of fourths. Play the chords in the right hand and the roots in the left; then practice the chords in the left hand while the right hand rests.

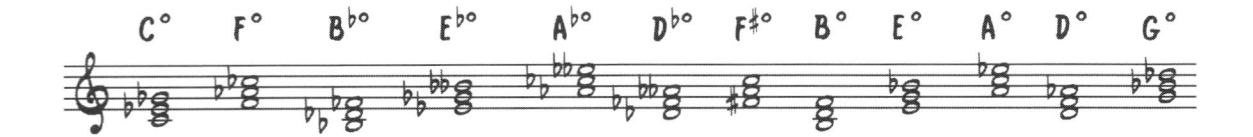

Exercise 1-6: Diminished Triads - Chromatic

Practice triads chromatically, ascending and descending. Play the chords in the right hand and the roots in the left; then practice the chords in the left hand while the right hand rests.

Simple Voicings   9

Exercise 1-7: Augmented Triads – Circle of Fourths

Practice triads by moving around the circle of fourths. Play the chords in the right hand and the roots in the left; then practice the chords in the left hand while the right hand rests.

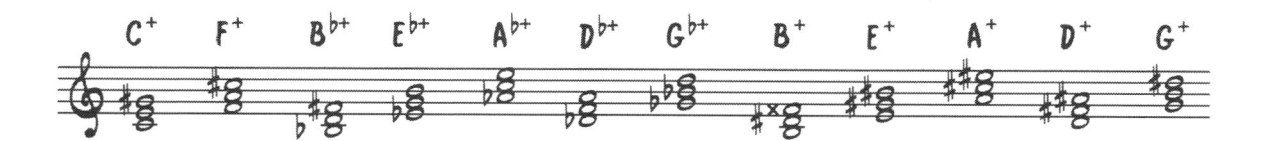

C⁺   F⁺   B♭⁺   E♭⁺   A♭⁺   D♭⁺   G♭⁺   B⁺   E⁺   A⁺   D⁺   G⁺

Exercise 1-8: Augmented Triads - Chromatic

Practice triads chromatically, ascending and descending. Play the chords in the right hand and the roots in the left; then practice the chords in the left hand while the right hand rests.

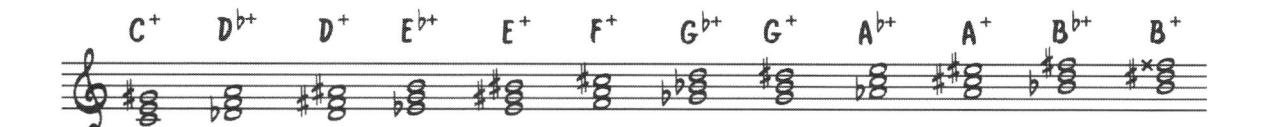

C⁺   D♭⁺   D⁺   E♭⁺   E⁺   F⁺   G♭⁺   G⁺   A♭⁺   A⁺   B♭⁺   B⁺

Exercise 1-9: All Triad Qualities

Random pattern, where only the first four chords are notated. These triads should be played with a metronome to measure your progress. Play the chords in the right hand and the roots in the left; then practice the chords in the left hand while the right hand rests. You should make up your own progression of random chords.

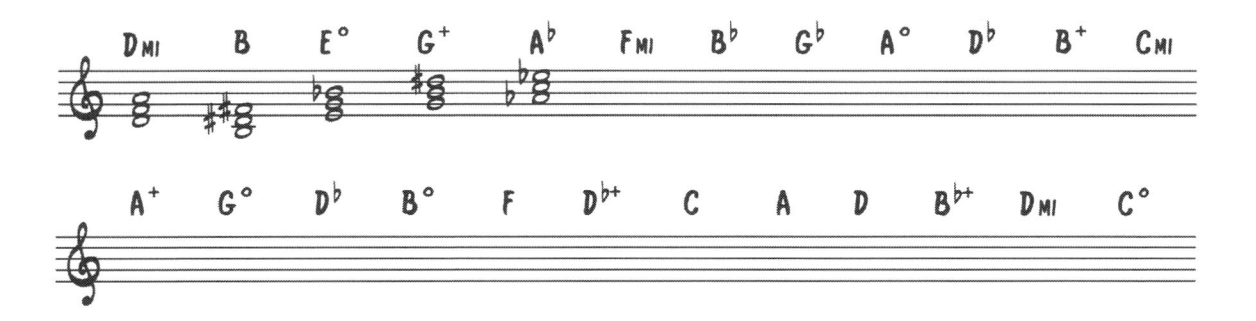

Dmi   B   E°   G⁺   A♭   Fmi   B♭   G♭   A°   D♭   B⁺   Cmi

A⁺   G°   D♭   B°   F   D♭⁺   C   A   D   B♭⁺   Dmi   C°

10 Part I: Voicings and Harmonic Progression

> *Exercise 1-10*: Diatonic Triads
>
> This exercise may require some review of a jazz theory text. In this exercise, the chords found on each scale degree, in every key, should be memorized, in major and minor. C major and minor, and F major and minor are provided to guide you. Each key will have this same progression of chord qualities, as each key is constructed as equals. <u>Minor keys present a unique challenge</u>, because of the three forms of minor scales and the resulting variability of the sixth and seventh degrees, as well as the melodic minor mode possibilities. Again, consultation with a jazz theory text is recommended. The minor key chord choices shown below reflect common usage, but are not the only possibilities. Play the chords in the right hand and the roots in the left; then practice the chords in the left hand while the right hand rests.

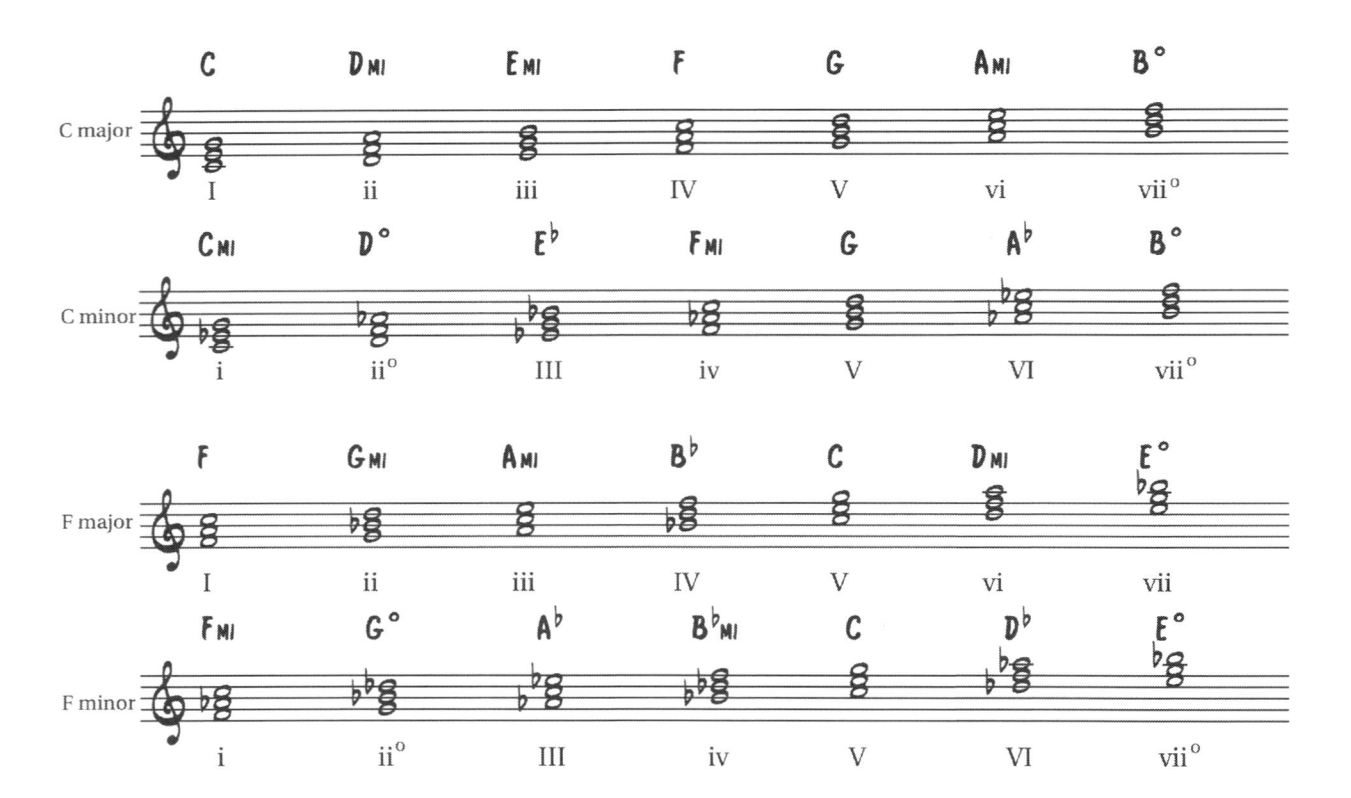

C major: C (I) — Dmi (ii) — Emi (iii) — F (IV) — G (V) — Ami (vi) — B° (vii°)

C minor: Cmi (i) — D° (ii°) — E♭ (III) — Fmi (iv) — G (V) — A♭ (VI) — B° (vii°)

F major: F (I) — Gmi (ii) — Ami (iii) — B♭ (IV) — C (V) — Dmi (vi) — E° (vii)

F minor: Fmi (i) — G° (ii°) — A♭ (III) — B♭mi (iv) — C (V) — D♭ (VI) — E° (vii°)

Inversions

Chords can be played in as many positions as there are chord tone members. Therefore, a triad can be played in three positions – with the root, third, or fifth on the bottom. While it is important to be aware of the bottom note of a chord (as is referenced often in music theory texts and courses), the resulting top note is critical for jazz pianists. One of the ways that we play jazz standards is to voice the melody under right hand chords. So thinking 'top-down' is a very important 'view' of jazz voicings. Example 1-4 includes an example of a C major triad in its three positions. These should be practiced in every key, with every triad chord quality.

Example 1-4 Major Triad Inversions

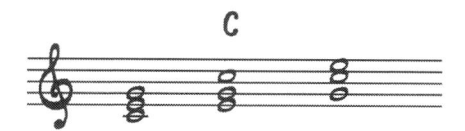

> ### Exercise 1-11: Triad Inversions
>
> Practice triad inversions with major, minor, augmented, and diminished qualities – all chords. Pay attention to the top note in particular, as that will be the focal point when harmonizing a melody. Play the chords in the right hand and the roots in the left; then practice the chords in the left hand while the right hand rests.

Seventh Chords

Most chords in jazz harmony are identified as some type of seventh chord. In fact, one could conclude that the basic structure of common-practice classical music is the triad and the basic structure of jazz harmony is the four-note chord, containing a seventh (or a substitute, as we'll see later). Since chords are built in thirds, it is a simple matter to stack another third on top of a triad, thereby adding the seventh above the root. There are six basic types: major seventh, dominant seventh, minor seventh, minor-major, half-diminished, and fully diminished. Expanding on the explanation of lead sheet notation, the following procedure is used for seventh chords: to identify seventh chords, think of the following: the word "major" always and only refers to the seventh (not the third). If the distance between the root and seventh is a major interval, then the abbreviation "ma" is required. (As noted above, there are various symbols used in this system, with little consistency). If the distance is a minor seventh, then the number 7 stands alone. The word "minor" always and only refers to the third (not the seventh). If the distance between the root and third is a minor interval, then the abbreviation "mi" is required. The exception is of course the diminished triad, which includes a minor third

12 Part I: Voicings and Harmonic Progression

but is notated with a small circle.   If the distance is a major third, then the letter name of the chord stands alone. Half-diminished chords are labeled with a slashed circle, or as a "mi♭5; the fully diminished seventh is identified by a circle with the number "7". The six seventh chords are shown in Example 1-5.

Example 1-5 Seventh Chord Construction

Seventh Chord Exercises

The exercises that follow are critical; seventh chord construction is the foundation of this music. These should be practiced by not only reading the exercises, but more importantly, ensuring that they are committed to memory. The chords flow around the circle of fourths. There are no chromatic or random exercises in this section, but these can certainly be added to your practice routine.

> **Exercise 1-12: Major Sevenths – Circle of Fourths**
>
> Practice seventh chords by moving around the circle of fourths. Play the chords in the right hand and the roots in the left; then practice the chords in the left hand while the right hand rests.

Simple Voicings 13

Exercise 1-13: Dominant Sevenths – Circle of Fourths

Practice seventh chords by moving around the circle of fourths. Play the chords in the right hand and the roots in the left; then practice the chords in the left hand while the right hand rests.

C7 F7 B♭7 E♭7 A♭7 D♭7 F#7 B7 E7 A7 D7 G7

Exercise 1-14: Minor Sevenths – Circle of Fourths

Practice seventh chords by moving around the circle of fourths. Play the chords in the right hand and the roots in the left; then practice the chords in the left hand while the right hand rests.

Cmi7 Fmi7 B♭mi7 E♭mi7 A♭mi7 D♭mi7 F#mi7 Bmi7 Emi7 Ami7 Dmi7 Gmi7

Exercise 1-15: Minor/Major Sevenths – Circle of Fourths

Practice seventh chords by moving around the circle of fourths. Play the chords in the right hand and the roots in the left; then practice the chords in the left hand while the right hand rests.

Cmi(ma7) Fmi(ma7) B♭mi(ma7) E♭mi(ma7) A♭mi(ma7) D♭mi(ma7) F#mi(ma7) Bmi(ma7) Emi(ma7) Ami(ma7) Dmi(ma7) Gmi(ma7)

14 Part I: Voicings and Harmonic Progression

> ### Exercise 1-16: Half Diminished Sevenths – Circle of Fourths
>
> Practice seventh chords by moving around the circle of fourths. Play the chords in the right hand and the roots in the left; then practice the chords in the left hand while the right hand rests.

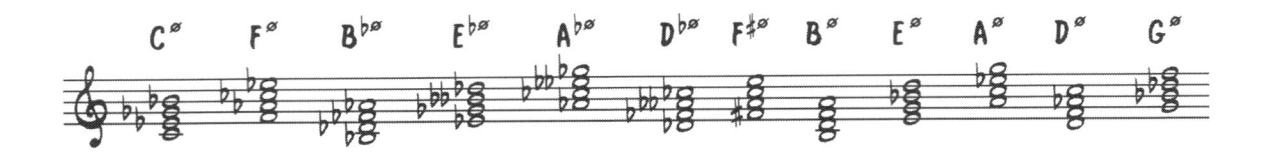

C⌀   F⌀   B♭⌀   E♭⌀   A♭⌀   D♭⌀   F♯⌀   B⌀   E⌀   A⌀   D⌀   G⌀

> ### Exercise 1-17: Diminished Sevenths – Circle of Fourths
>
> Practice seventh chords by moving around the circle of fourths. Play the chords in the right hand and the roots in the left; then practice the chords in the left hand while the right hand rests.

C°7   F°7   B♭°7   D♯°7   G♯°7   C♯°7   F♯°7   B°7   E°7   A°7   D°7   G°7

Exercise 1-18 below re-visits the diatonic exercise first presented in the triad section, and you'll see the complication of working within minor is increased. As before, C and F major and minor are used to illustrate the diatonic system, but this time as seventh chords on each scale degree. The chords in minor represent the most common usage of these diatonic chords, but there are more possibilities – and it may be a good time to consult a jazz theory text. (For example, note that the tonic chord in C minor – C mi7 - includes a B♭ and the G7 includes a B♮). Finally, the Roman numerals match that of the triad example, with the exception of the fully diminished and half diminished symbol.

Simple Voicings 15

Exercise 1-18: Diatonic Sevenths

Practice in all keys. Play the chords in the right hand and the roots in the left; then practice the chords in the left hand while the right hand rests.

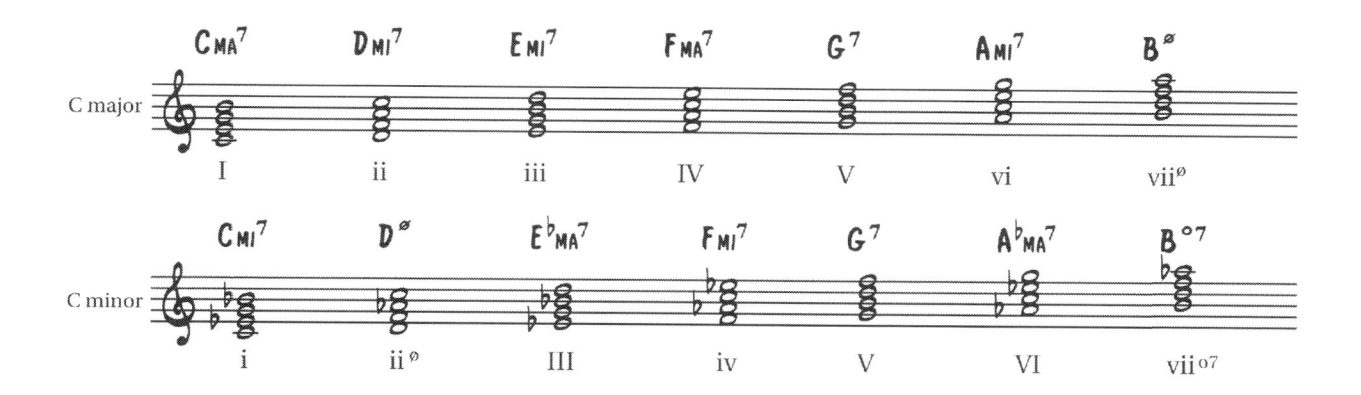

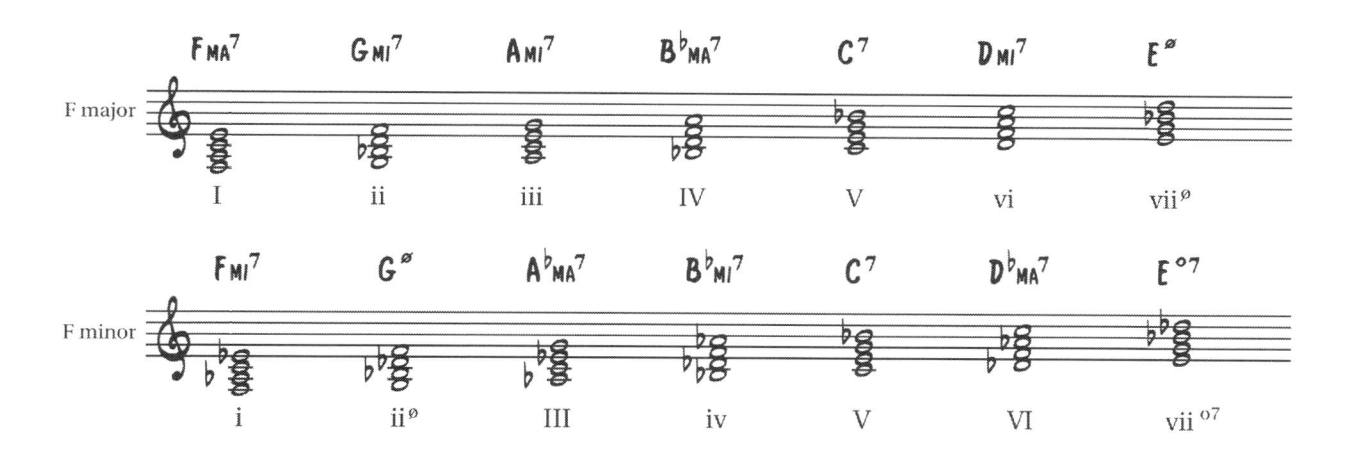

C major: CMA7 (I), DMI7 (ii), EMI7 (iii), FMA7 (IV), G7 (V), AMI7 (vi), Bø (viiø)

C minor: CMI7 (i), Dø (iiø), E♭MA7 (III), FMI7 (iv), G7 (V), A♭MA7 (VI), B°7 (vii°7)

F major: FMA7 (I), GMI7 (ii), AMI7 (iii), B♭MA7 (IV), C7 (V), DMI7 (vi), Eø (viiø)

F minor: FMI7 (i), Gø (iiø), A♭MA7 (III), B♭MI7 (iv), C7 (V), D♭MA7 (VI), E°7 (vii°7)

16 Part I: Voicings and Harmonic Progression

Seventh Chord Inversions

Example 1-6 illustrates the four positions of a seventh chord. Like the triad exercise in Exercise 1-4, practice seventh chord inversions. Again, this is a critical skill for harmonizing melodies.

Example 1-6 Seventh Chord Inversions

> *Exercise 1-19*: **Seventh Chord Inversions**
>
> Practice seventh chord inversions with major, dominant, minor, half-diminished, and fully-diminished qualities – all chords. When playing in your right hand, pay attention to the top note in particular, as that will be the focal point when harmonizing a melody.

The *Guided Learning Tunes* are illustrated in Example 1-7 and 1-8 with root position seventh chords in the left hand. There are no voice-leading considerations or appropriate rhythms used – just the chords are notated.

Example 1-7 Guided Learning Tunes I – Left Hand Root Positions Chords

Example 1-8 Guided Learning Tune II – Left Hand Root Positions Chords

Guide Tone Chord Voicings

The word "guide" has several meanings. The term refers to a person who leads or directs, or a device for steadying or directing motion. When we refer to "guide tones" in music, we're talking about something that provides a person with *guiding* information. There are various musical elements that guide the listener's ears, providing the information to understand the content. Harmony is an extremely important element, and will be discussed below.

Jazz pianists normally do not play chords in simple root position, because more color and contrast is demanded by the music in most cases. Root position is also avoided because the *connection* of chords, also known as *voice-leading*, is critical. As more complex harmonies are explored, it is important to understand the tones that must be present, as well as those that can

18 Part I: Voicings and Harmonic Progression

be omitted, or substituted, with more colorful choices. These concepts will be covered in subsequent chapters. For now, the goal is to express chords with the minimum of notes, connecting them properly, and ultimately building more complex voicings – beyond root position – in later exercises. Emphasizing thirds and sevenths in a progression of chords provides the most basic method of connecting chords effectively. The fifth remains the same (that is, perfect) among chords that do not have an altered fifth (like diminished and augmented chords), and the root can be separated from the chord by playing it in the left hand (or leaving that tone to the bassist). Therefore, it is important to conceive of and practice playing chords with only the third and seventh present in the right hand with the root in the left.

Guide Tone Chord Positions

The third or seventh can appear on the bottom of the right hand, since there are the only chords tones present. There are letter 'names' associated with these two positions which will used throughout the text. *A position* refers to when the third is on the bottom of the right hand, *B position* refers to when the seventh is on the bottom. Example 1-9 illustrates these voicings.

Example 1-9 *Guide Voicing Construction*

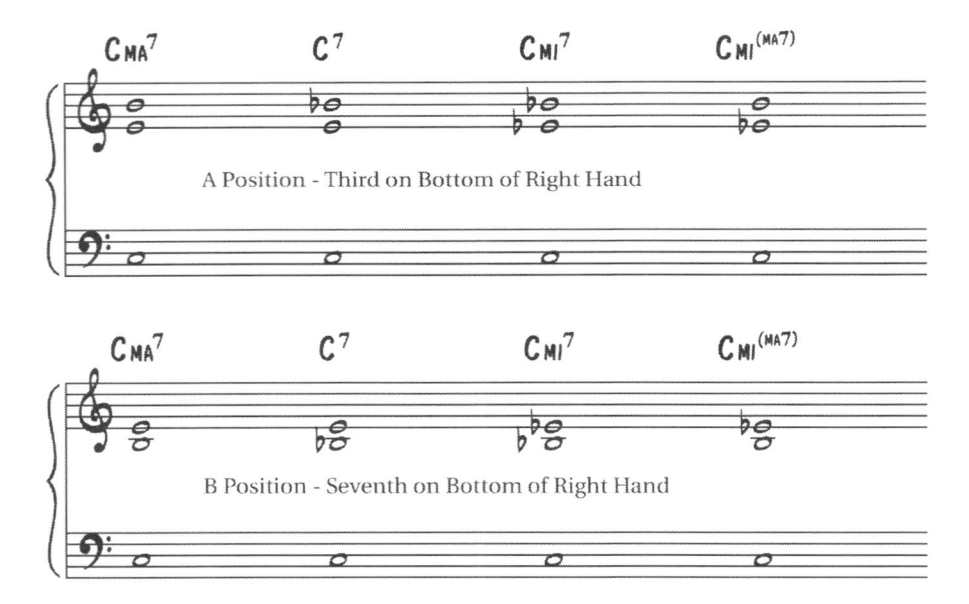

[Musical notation: Four chords CMA7, C7, CMI7, CMI(MA7) shown in A Position - Third on Bottom of Right Hand]

[Musical notation: Four chords CMA7, C7, CMI7, CMI(MA7) shown in B Position - Seventh on Bottom of Right Hand]

Example 1-10 illustrates major seventh chords in all keys, moving around the circle of fourths on the following page, first in A position, and below that in B position.

Example 1-10 Guide Tone Voicings – Major Sevenths

Exercise 1-20: Guide Tone Voicings

Practice guide tone voicings as shown above in Example 1-10. Although only major sevenths are illustrated, practice dominant sevenths, minor sevenths, and minor/major sevenths as well. Consult Example 1-9 to observe how to change the seventh and third for each chord quality.

A fundamental motion in music is the behavior of the thirds and sevenths in a circle of fourths progression. The following example illustrates the motion, as the seventh moves to third in one 'voice', while the opposite occurs in the other 'voice'. Thus A position voicings move to B position voicings, then back to A, etc. It is critical that this motion be thoroughly understood before diatonic progressions – like the ii-V-I – are practiced. Example 1-11 below illustrates this movement, starting with the A position and then the B position, and Exercise 1-21 outlines the process for practicing this important motion.

20 Part I: Voicings and Harmonic Progression

Example 1-11 Guide Tone Voicings - Major Sevenths, Alternating Positions

> **Exercise 1-21:** Guide Tone Voicings: Proper Voice Leading
>
> Use the major seventh voicings in Example 1-11 as a model to practice major, dominant, and minor seventh chords using proper voice leading.

Harmonizing a Melody

As mentioned above, in the triad section of this chapter, one of the most common and effective ways for jazz pianists to arrange a standard is to place the melody on the top of right hand voicings. This approach resembles how arrangers harmonize a melody when working with horn players or vocalists. This homophonic method, where the harmony follows the contour of the melody, works well for many styles and tempos including solo piano ballad playing; a solo piano setting where the left hand functions like a bass player, playing idiomatic swing and Latin bass lines; and ensemble playing (with a bassist present), where the hands combine in a variety of ways – 'locked hands', 'shout style', and others. (These topics will be described in Chapters 9 and 10). Example 1-12 illustrates the right-hand harmonization of *GLT I* using only guide tones. Note that the third and sevenths are added when the chord appears under the appropriate melody note; thereafter the melody is played as a single line. This approach makes this type of playing quite simple. Also note that when the melody is one of the guide tones – either the third or the seventh – the right hand only plays two notes; when the melody is a non-guide tone (like the fifth for example), three notes are played. Finally, note that the D half diminished chord in the third measure is incomplete because the lowered fifth is not there. It is present in the following measure, however, since the lowered fifth – the A♭ - is in the melody.

Example 1-12 Guide Tone Harmonization of GLT I

Exercise 1-22: Guide Tone Voicings – Harmonizing Standard Melodies

Use the method illustrated above in Example 1-12 to harmonize standard melodies. Place thirds and sevenths under the melody of tunes such as *Satin Doll, All the Things You Are, Here's that Rainy Day,* and other standards with conventional chord progressions. The left hand should only play the chord roots, and the melody should be harmonized primarily where it corresponds with first sounding of a new chord.

2

Simple Harmonic Progression

Harmonic function in jazz is governed by the interconnectedness of melodic lines and harmonic motion. These two forces provide momentum, variety, contrast, and intensity. Theorists describe a hierarchy of harmonic 'areas' that govern tonal harmony: tonic, dominant, and pre-dominant. While these harmonic areas contain potentially multiple chords (for example, the pre-dominant area can be populated by both the ii and IV), the chords most relevant for jazz musicians are ii (pre-dominant), V (dominant), and I (tonic). This progression – the ii-V-I – is composed of two falling fifth motions – ii to V, and V to I. A very simple, yet instructive, way to see this harmonic motion is through the use of guide tone voicings. Example 2-1 illustrates the progression.

Example 2-1 Guide Tone voicings: ii-V-I in C Major

Along with the strong root movement of falling fifths, the progression also features smooth voice leading. Note that in the example above the thirds move to sevenths, sevenths to thirds – exactly like the motion in Example 1-11, where the A and B chord positions alternate with one another. While Example 1-11 features the same chord quality throughout, the ii-V-I is *diatonic*, in that the three chords all belong to the key of the I. Example 2-2 illustrates the ii-V-I progression in all major keys, moving around the circle of fourths.

24   Part I: Voicings and Harmonic Progression

Example 2-2 *ii-V-I – Major keys, guide tone voicings, circle of fourths*

> ***Exercise 2-1:* The ii-V-I Progression, Guide Tones**
>
> Practice the ii-V-I progression as illustrated in Example 2-2.

As mentioned earlier, minor keys present a unique problem, and the ii-V-I progression offers an excellent opportunity to explore how composers and improvisers combine the various options related to minor. Because more tones are required to express the progression in minor (specifically, a flatted fifth in the ii chord), the minor ii-V-I will be addressed in the chapter 4, where more complex chords are introduced.

3

Four-Way Close Voicings, Tonal Clusters, and Chord Tone Substitution

As we distribute chord tones (or "voice" them) we can stack them consecutively in thirds, we can create gaps between some of the chord tones and create wider structures, or we can place some of the tones next to one another. Chords that are within the range of one octave are said to be in a *close position*. If the chord has four different tones, it is commonly referred to as *four-way close*. Chords that are not consecutively stacked and exceed the interval of one octave are said to be in *open position*. Tackling close voicings first will make the open voicing section in Chapter 5 much simpler to understand. Obviously, chords can be constructed of more than four notes, in both close and open position and these voicings often include colorful tonal clusters. The 'rules', for lack of a better term, will first be focused on four note chords in close position, and chords with more tones will conclude the chapter.

Four-Way Close Voicings

As mentioned above, a chord containing four separate notes that reside within the range of an octave is called *four-way close*. This voicing is the most common structure used by jazz arrangers and pianists, and we'll see that it is the most useful way to understand jazz harmony. Root position seventh chords are in four-way close, so we've already dealt with this idea; they are illustrated in Example 1-5.

Upper Extensions

By adding more thirds to the basic seventh chords, the ninth, eleventh, and thirteenth notes appear. These are called 'upper extensions'. The notation guidelines are as follows: <u>when upper extensions are added, the number of the highest extension is used to identify the chord.</u> The remaining tones are available for the pianist, but often not all are used. Deciding tones to eliminate will be described below in the discussion of substituting chord tones. When the extensions are major intervals above the root, or perfect in the case of the fourth and eleventh, the numbers stand alone without modification – regardless of the key. Remember - the words major and minor are only utilized as identifiers of the seventh and third and are not used to describe upper extensions. If upper extensions are raised or lowered, sharp or flat (or plus or minus) symbols are used. Finally, a few words about the fifth: beyond the root, third, and seventh, the fifth is not a part of the 'major/minor' labeling system of identifying the basic

28 Part I: Voicings and Harmonic Progression

seventh chord types, as those words refer to the seventh and third, respectively. The fifth can be raised or lowered, however, and in those cases, the fifth is labeled with a sharp or flat symbol in front of it. Example 3-1 illustrates how the entire system functions, with explanations provided for each. All of the possible chord tones are included, and as mentioned above, in many cases all tones would not be used in an actual musical setting:

Example 3-1 *Upper Extensions*

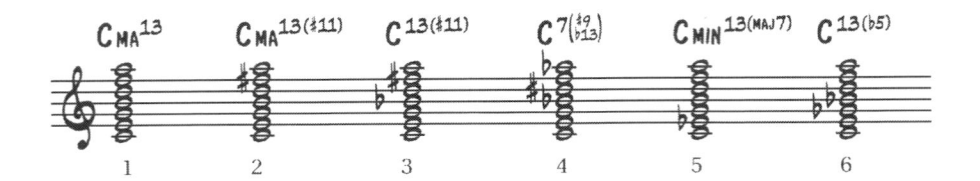

C_{MA}^{13} $C_{MA}^{13(\sharp 11)}$ $C^{13(\sharp 11)}$ $C^{7\binom{\sharp 9}{\flat 13}}$ $C_{MIN}^{13(MAJ7)}$ $C^{13(\flat 5)}$

1. The thirteenth is the highest unaltered tone, so that number is used in the symbol. It has a major third, so the word 'minor' is not there; it has a major seventh, so the word 'major' ('ma') is needed.

2. This example is identical to number 1, but the eleventh is raised, which is indicated.

3. This example again has the thirteenth as its highest chord tone. The eleventh is again raised. This chord has a major third, so the word 'minor' is not needed, but has a minor seventh (the B♭), so the word 'major' is omitted. (Because the basic structure has a major third and minor seventh, it is in the 'dominant seventh' family of chords).

4. This example, also a dominant seventh-type structure, illustrates a chord with a flatted thirteenth. In this case, the highest unaltered chord tone is the seventh, so it is used in the symbol. It has a sharp ninth and a flatted thirteenth, which are indicated. (Important: the 11th is indeed there, and is the highest unaltered tone; but we'll learn shortly that this note is often not used in chords with major thirds).

5. This example illustrates a "minor-major" type chord, but with the thirteenth as its highest unaltered tone, the number thirteen is used in the symbol.

6. This example illustrates the alteration of the fifth. It is a dominant seventh type of chord, with the thirteenth as its highest chord tone.

Since chords are usually identified as some type of seventh chord, the actual chord tones chosen by the player involve a process called 'chord tone substitution'. These substituted chord tones are also commonly referred to as *alterations.*

Chord Tone Substitutions

Most chords in the jazz idiom are expressed simply by indicating three elements: the root, the quality of the chord, and the number seven. A seasoned jazz performer can embellish that basic chord symbol by adding and/or changing chord tones using upper extensions to express a richer, more colorful sound. These musicians understand that the seventh chord designation is merely a point of departure and that upper extensions, as well as the fourth and sixth, play a vital role in jazz harmony. Simple root position seventh chords that have only the fundamental tones (i.e., the root, third, fifth, and seventh) are actually the exception rather than the rule.

The richness of jazz harmony involves a hierarchy of substitution possibilities for these four tones. For this reason, it is best to think of each of these chord tones not as required tones, as you may be led to believe from the chord symbol, but rather as chord tones that are almost always replaced, or substituted, according to rather specific guidelines. However, there are instances where more than four notes can be present. (A chord can theoretically contain all seven tones of a scale). Chord tone substitution as discussed here involves a limit of four tones – so that some must be eliminated to bring in more colorful choices.

Let's first pair each of these fundamental chord tones with possible substitutions, illustrated below:

- The root can be replaced by the ninth.
- The third can be replaced by the fourth.
- The fifth can be replaced by the thirteenth or eleventh.
- The seventh can be replaced by the sixth.

I mentioned above that there are rules regarding these substitution possibilities, and these rules are dependent upon three important considerations: the chord quality, the key that you're in, and the tone color you want. We'll discuss how keys affect the substitution rules in a moment. First let's explore chord tone substitutions in the context of chord quality and tone color.

The "color" of a chord describes the variations of darkness and brightness. A dark chord will contain more dissonance and therefore increased instability – the ear will hear it as a chord that should go somewhere, or 'resolve'. A bright chord tends to be more at rest. Alterations of the upper extensions (and the fifth) will encourage these tendencies.

The upper extensions, along with the fourth and sixth, are all major intervals above the root (in the case of the ninth, sixth, and thirteenth) or perfect intervals (in the case of the fourth and eleventh). However, the chord symbol can indicate alterations of these tones (i.e., ♯11). Ninths can be lowered or raised, elevenths can be raised, but not lowered (a flatted eleventh is the equivalent of a major third), and thirteenths can be lowered but not raised (a raised thirteenth is the equivalent of a minor seventh). Also, the thirteenth and sixth are the same note an octave apart, as are the eleventh and fourth and the ninth and second; a "2" is sometimes seen in a symbol where the second, or ninth, is added to a triad. With this background knowledge, examine Example 3-2 which lists chord tone substitutions for ma7, dom7, mi7, mi7♭5, and diminished 7 chords. You'll notice that even though the ninth, eleventh, and thirteenth are considered upper extensions (i.e., above the seventh) they are notated in the same octave as the fundamental chord tones. Note that the ninth/second, thirteenth/sixth, and eleventh/fourth substitution possibilities have been organized by "type". And finally, these are not voicings to be practiced, but studied and understood. This is simply a chart that outlines the possibilities. Actual voicings are presented later in this chapter.

Example 3-2 Chord Tone Substitution Chart

By reading the chart from left to right, the following points can be summarized:

• The ninth can replace the root in all chord qualities. The ninth is easily the most frequent chord tone substitution.

• Raised and lowered ninths can replace the root only in a dominant, because of the desire to make this chord more unstable (and heighten its resolution).

• The thirteenth can place the fifth in the major, dominant, and minor chords.

• Lowered thirteenths can replace the fifth only in a dominant seventh (for the same reason as cited above for the raised and lowered ninths – increased instability).

• The sixth can replace the seventh in a major or minor seventh. This makes a very effective tonic chord – especially when the root is in the melody, as in the last melody tone of a tune.

- The raised eleventh can replace the fifth in a major and a dominant seventh. These are sometimes labeled as flatted fifths, e.g. Cma7(♭5).

- The suspended fourth can replace the third only in a dominant seventh. The eleventh can replace the fifth in a minor seventh.

- Half-diminished chords with major ninths are generated from the locrian sharp two melodic minor mode.

- Diminished sevenths are unique, since they are symmetrical (a series of stacked minor thirds); a tone placed a whole step above any of the chord tones will function and sound like a ninth.

All this leads to these questions: why use these particular substitutions? When should I use a thirteenth? Should I use it in conjunction with a ninth? An altered ninth? As was mentioned above, chord tone substitutions provide a richer, more colorful sound. They also provide more dissonance, and *dissonant chords tend to drive the music forward toward a resolution.* For example, the dominant seventh chord, when functioning as a V chord (which is its usual role) <u>requires</u> substitute chord tones, because the chord needs a degree of instability as it leads to a resolution. The thirteenth provides that dissonance, as it clashes (in a good way) with the seventh, because the thirteenth and seventh are separated by a dissonant major seventh (or by a half step if in the same octave).

Important Considerations: What Key Are You In? And Where is the Melody?

The substitution chart above is quite concise in summarizing the substitution options. However, it does contain some unavoidable flaws – the overall key or the "key of the moment" (involving secondary function), the mode use (such as the important melodic minor modes), nor the melody being harmonized are taken into consideration. For example, the appropriate thirteenth of the V chord in the key of C minor is a <u>flatted</u> thirteenth (E♭) to match the key. So the tonality will govern what you utilize as substitutes. This, however, actually makes things easier. The key provides a structure that guides the pianist toward particular decisions. Additionally, while it is fine to place a chord tone a whole step below a melodic tone, a half step is normally avoided. This serves to limit your chord substitution choices. Two common examples create unwanted half steps:

- Minor sevenths when the third is the melodic tone: Replacing the root with the ninth creates a half step (the melody note E♭ in a C minor chord - the third, is adjacent to the ninth, a D).

- Dominant sevenths when the seventh is the melodic tone: Replacing the fifth with the thirteenth creates a half step (the melody note B♭ in a C7 - the seventh, is adjacent to the thirteenth, an A). In both these cases, the basic chord tones would be preferable.

32 Part I: Voicings and Harmonic Progression

Four-way Close Exercises Using Chord Tone Substitution

The following exercises contain four-way close voicings with either the third on the bottom ('A' position), or the seventh on the bottom ('B' position). It is important to understand that four note structures could be placed with any of the chord tones on the bottom – A and B are the most common. However, when harmonizing a melody in the right hand, the melody will determine what position, or inversion, the chord will be placed. For now, the A and B positions will be used to illustrate various chord tone substitutions. The exercises follow the circle of fourths, but could be practiced in other ways: randomly; diatonically (all chords of a single key), in minor thirds or major thirds, etc. They are shown in only the treble clef (without bass clef root) to save space. Only major, dominant, and minor sevenths are illustrated. Half and fully diminished chords as well as minor-major sevenths should be drilled in the same manner.

> *Exercise 3-1:* **Four Way Close Voicings: A & B Positions, Major, Dominant, and Minor Sevenths – Circle of Fourths**
>
> Practice the chords below. Be aware of each and every chord tone as you play the exercise. Play the chords in the right hand and the roots in the left; then practice the chords in the left hand while the right hand rests.

A position:

[Musical notation showing four-way close voicings in A position following circle of fourths, with three rows: Major 7th chords (CMA7, FMA7, B♭MA7, E♭MA7, A♭MA7, D♭MA7, F♯MA7, BMA7, EMA7, AMA7, DMA7, GMA7) labeled "9 subs for root"; Dominant 7th chords (C7, F7, B♭7, E♭7, A♭7, D♭7, F♯7, B7, E7, A7, D7, G7) labeled "13 subs for 5, 9 subs for root"; Minor 7th chords (CMI7, FMI7, B♭MI7, E♭MI7, A♭MI7, D♭MI7, F♯MI7, BMI7, EMI7, AMI7, DMI7, GMI7) labeled "9 subs for root"]

Four-Way Close, Tonal Clusters, and Chord Tone Substitution

B position:

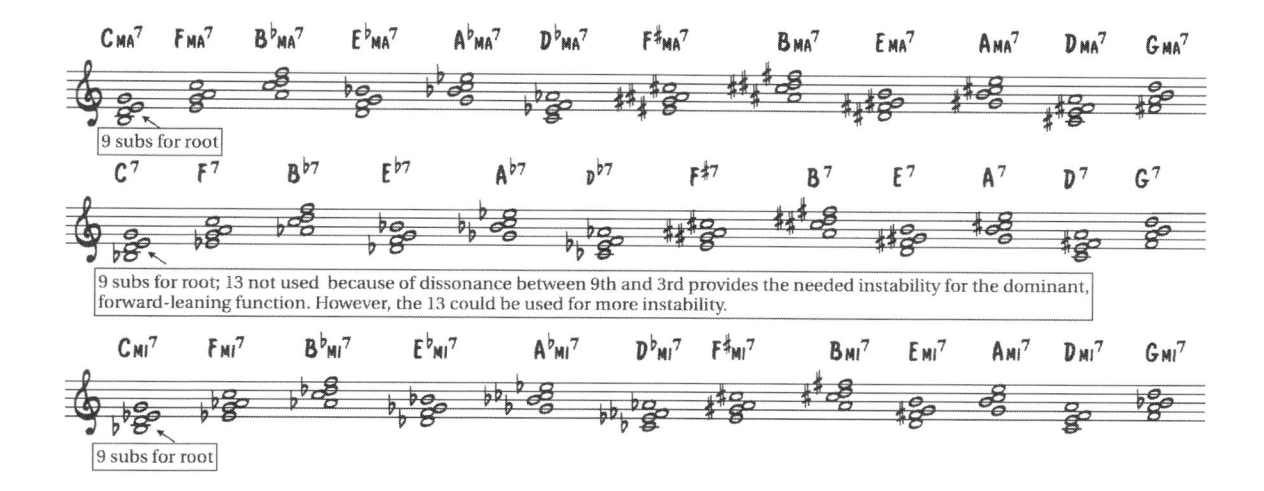

[9 subs for root]

[9 subs for root; 13 not used because of dissonance between 9th and 3rd provides the needed instability for the dominant, forward-leaning function. However, the 13 could be used for more instability.]

[9 subs for root]

Chord Tone Substitution in Practice: The Dominant Seventh Chord

While specific examples of chord tone substitution will be discussed throughout the following pages – especially when we arrive at more complex harmonic motion – it will be useful at this point to offer a specific example of how the all-important dominant seventh chord is affected by substituting chord tones in various situations. The dominant seventh chord's normal function is as a V chord in major and minor keys, resolving down a perfect fifth – but it is seen elsewhere where it doesn't resolve by a fifth. Examples include its use as a tritone substitute, as a tonic in a blues, as a secondary dominant leading to a minor seventh with the same root (think of the A section of *Take the A Train:* D7-Dmi7, in measures 3-5), or simply as a non-functional chord, perhaps in a modal-type composition. A review of these jazz theory concepts might be useful at this point by consulting a jazz theory book. With this in mind, the dominant seventh should employ chord tone substitution as follows:

1. Dominant seventh functioning as a V in a F major:

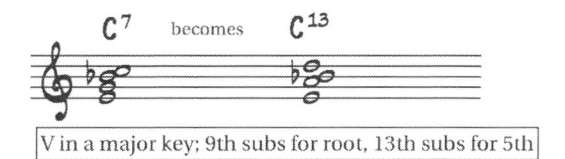

[V in a major key; 9th subs for root, 13th subs for 5th]

34   Part I: Voicings and Harmonic Progression

2. Dominant seventh functioning as a V in F minor:

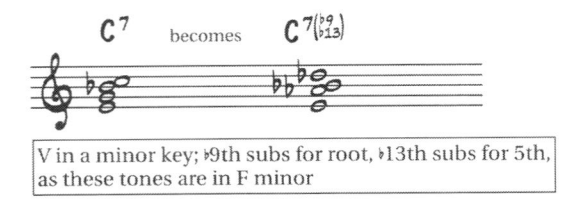

[musical notation: C7 becomes C7(♭9,♭13)]

V in a minor key; ♭9th subs for root, ♭13th subs for 5th, as these tones are in F minor

3. Dominant seventh as a non-resolving dominant:

[musical notation: C7 becomes C9(♯11)]

V that does not resolve, so bright tones are best; 9th subs for root, ♯11th subs for 5th, as these tones are in the lydian/dominant melodic minor mode

4. Dominant seventh functioning as a V in F major, but implying diminished harmony:

[musical notation: C7 becomes C13(♭9)]

V in a major key; ♭9th subs for root, 13th subs for 5th. This implies the half/whole diminished scale.

Placing the Voicings Within a Musical Context

Example 3-3 is meant to resemble a 'jam session' progression, where only a couple of chords of the same quality are played many times (like in a "garage band" setting). This can be an effective alternative to working through all twelve chords, creating a more focused practice routine. The exercise is also meant to resemble a more 'musical' setting, where it should sound like you are 'jamming' and creating music rather than just practicing. Note that the chords move down in major seconds, and that four chords are drilled (plus a final chord that 'turns around' the progression). The left hand performs a standard *bossa nova* bass line (which will be re-visited in Chapter 9).

Example 3-3: "Jam Session" Repetitive Progression – Musical Context

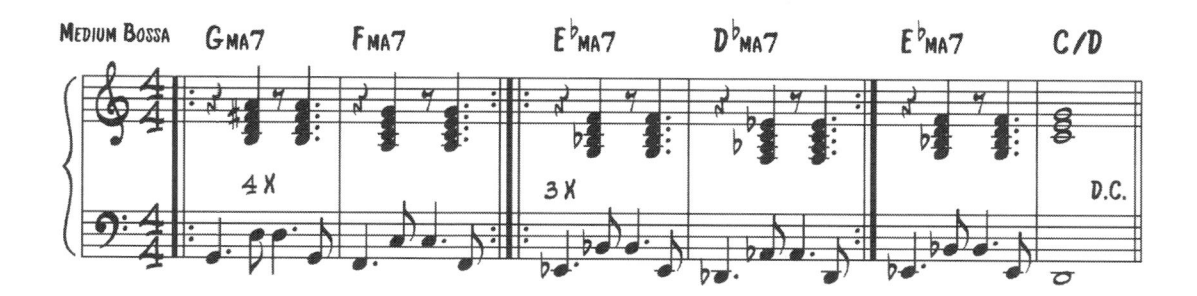

The example above is notated with major ninth chords in the A position. These could be played with any chord quality, (i.e., Gmi7-Fmi7, E♭mi7, D♭mi7) and in various positions (i.e., third on the bottom of the right hand, seventh, fifth, or ninth – or a combination of all of them).

Example 3-4 illustrates a version where a variety of chord positions and rhythms are played. This is quite challenging, as this type of playing requires advanced hand independence, where the left hand is providing the *bossa* nova foundation. As you listen to the recording and perform the exercise, notice that a melody is created by the top note of the chords. As was mentioned in Chapter 3, harmonizing a melody by visualizing a chord voicing from the top down is critical for jazz pianists. For this reason, playing chords in a variety of positions (beyond the A and B positions) is an extremely important skill.

36 Part I: Voicings and Harmonic Progression

Example 3-4 "Jam Session" Repetitive Progression – Varied Inversions and Rhythms

Since four chords are drilled, a third of all possible chords are included (because there are only twelve). In order to take full advantage of this exercise, it should be transposed so that there is overlap with chords already learned, thereby further drilling and repeating. If one were to start on a different chord, F for example, the chord sequence would be F – E♭, then D♭ – B, then a turnaround chord of C. This simple idea, where repetition and music-making are emphasized, can be an effective tool to add to circle of fourth exercises. The exercise below includes all of the possibilities; note that since the progression moves in descending major seconds, there are two resulting 'sets', based upon the two whole tone scales.

> ***Exercise 3-2:*** **"Jam Session" Progression. Play this progression illustrated in Example 3-3, using major, dominant, and minor sevenths. Utilize the following order of keys:**
>
> Set 1:
>
> G – F - E♭ – D♭ - C/D (turnaround)….then F-E♭ - D♭ – B - B♭/C (turnaround)….then
>
> E♭ - D♭ - B – A - A♭/B♭ (turnaround)…then D♭ – B – A – G – G♭/A♭ (turnaround)…then
>
> B – A – G – F – E/F♯ (turnaround)…then A – G – F – E♭ – D/E (turnaround)
>
> Set 2:
>
> C – B♭ – A♭ – G♭ – F/G (turnaround)…then B♭ – A♭ – G♭ – E – E♭/F (turnaround)…then
>
> A♭ – G♭ – E – D – D♭/E♭ (turnaround)…then G♭ – E – D – C – B/D♭ (turnaround)…then
>
> E – D – C – B♭ – A/B (turnaround)…then D – C – B♭ – A♭ – G/A (turnaround)

Example 3-5 illustrates *Guided Learning Tune I* with four-way close voicings under the melody, played in the right hand. This would be the manner in which a solo pianist could perform the tune – all elements are here: melody and harmony are in the right hand and the bass note chord roots are in the left hand.

Example 3-5 GLT I with Four-Way Close Voicings Harmonizing the Melody

(musical notation)

Major 9th included - derived from the locrian #2 melodic minor mode

Notice that there are ninths and thirteenths used as chord tone substitutions for most of the chords. The G7(♭9) chord in measure four is harmonized with a flatted thirteenth because the E♭ is part of the C minor tonality. Finally, note the major ninth used in the D half diminished chord – this is derived from the locrian♯2 mode. Again consult a jazz theory textbook if you need to refresh your knowledge of the melodic minor mode system.

Close Position Voicings With Tonal Clusters

As mentioned at the beginning of this chapter, close position voicings can include more than the standard four notes – in fact, a chord could conceivably contain seven notes – all the notes of a scale. (Or – five notes of a pentatonic scale). Moving beyond the four-note structure while remaining within an octave span will result in tonal clusters. A tonal cluster is formed with three adjacent notes of a scale. It is extremely important to be aware of the key of the moment as you employ these voicings, as well as the mode occurring for each chord. Example 3-6 illustrates a very simple voicing with a cluster – a major and minor triad with an added ninth. This chord is commonly found in popular music (and is demonstrated in a comping pattern in Chapter 9). It is designated with an 'add 9' symbol (without the word 'add' the chord would contain a seventh) but is also sometimes labeled 'C2'.

Example 3-6 Close Position Voicing – Triad with added ninth

Example 3-7 illustrates an expanded use of clusters. Clusters can be derived from seven note scales (i.e., major, minor, modes), but also pentatonic scales, and five note chords within an octave are common. The example illustrates a five note Cmin11 voicing, in 'B' position (seventh on the bottom), containing all of the tones of a C minor pentatonic scale.

Example 3-7 Close Position Voicing with Clusters Derived from a Pentatonic Scale

The Dmi11 chord in Example 3-8 is in 'A' position (third on the bottom) and contains six notes. The chord tones are (from the bottom to the top) the third-eleventh-fifth-seventh-root-ninth. This beautiful chord would be difficult to transpose because it is dependent upon the thumb striking more than one note (this is possible with white key clusters). If the chord was to be played in the right hand, the thumb would strike the two bottom tones; if played in the left hand, the thumb would strike the top two tones.

Example 3-8 Close Position Voicing with Clusters – Six Notes

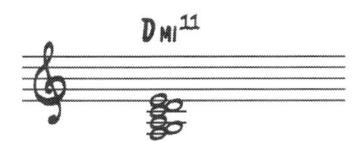

Example 3-9 illustrates a variety of close position voicings that contain clusters. While they are written so that most of the notes are on the staff, these voicings tend to sound best with

40 Part I: Voicings and Harmonic Progression

middle C serving as a mid-point. Note the 8va symbol below the staff. Also, these voicings could be paired with a variety of roots beyond what is indicated here. For example, the first chord Gmi11, could also function as a C7sus, a B♭ma7, an E♭ma7(♯11), among others.

Example 3-9 Close Position Voicings with Clusters – Various Chord Qualities

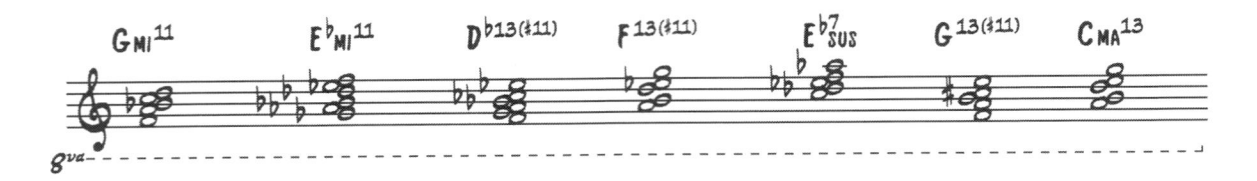

As long as the chord tone substitution process is understood, as well as the modal system, the pianist should attempt to add clusters, with some on the top and bottom and some in the middle of the voicing, as seen in the examples above. While chord function could still be governing the harmony, this process has more to do with a desired sonority for each chord rather than function. Try playing four note chords and simply add extra tones and listen to the effect – and add these to your voicing choices. These types of sounds will be illustrated again, at the end of the next chapter, where these complex sonorities are illustrated as they move from one to another.

> **Exercise 3-3: Close Position Voicings with Added Clusters**
>
> Experiment with close position voicings with added clusters. Listen carefully for the effect being created. Begin with the voicings illustrated in Examples 3-6, 3-7, 3-8, and 3-9, and experiment with your own.

Advanced Harmonic Progression: Four-Way Close Voicings

This chapter expands upon the simple harmonic progression introduced in Chapter 2 where the ii-V-I progression was presented as guide tone voicings. The motion of the thirds and sevenths was explored; now the ii-V-I progression will be examined using four-way close voicings, where the other chord tones will need to move appropriately, using proper voice-leading. Unlike in Chapter 2, these progressions will be presented in both major and minor. Additionally, a secondary dominant, the V of ii, will be utilized to create a repeating cycle and provide an opportunity to briefly explore the important role of secondary function. Obviously there are many more chord movements beyond the ii-V-I. Examples include back cycling (which is just an expansion of the ii-V-I progression, as it is also constructed of falling fifths); rhythm changes, blues substitutions, the Coltrane matrix, and modal interchange progressions are just a few possibilities. By focusing on the ii-V-I progression, however, proper voice-leading procedures can be examined and perfected, and this knowledge can be brought to other, more complex progressions.

Four-Way Close ii-V-I

In introducing the ii-V-I using only guide tone voicings, we learned that thirds and sevenths alternate with one another as the progression unfolds. By using four-way close voicings, and by employing common chord tone substitutions, we can conclude the following:

1. Thirds and sevenths alternate with one another.

2. Roots and fifths (and their substitutes, ninths and thirteenths) alternate with one another.

Example 4-1 provides an illustration, with ninths subbing for roots in all three chords, and a thirteenth subbing for the fifth in the G7 chord. These chord tone substitutions were summarized in Example 3-2.

42 Part I: Voicings and Harmonic Progression

Example 4-1 *Voicing Leading in the Four-Way Close ii-V-I Progression, A-B-A Positions*

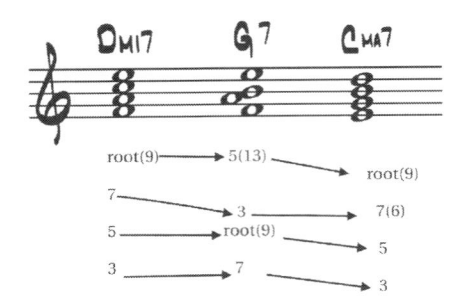

```
Dmi7       G7        Cma7
```

root(9) ──→ 5(13) ──→ root(9)
7 ─────────→ 3 ─────→ 7(6)
5 ─────→ root(9) ───→ 5
3 ─────────→ 7 ─────→ 3

Note that the chord labels are basic, as would likely be seen in a fake book. The chord tone substitutes illustrated are common, but not the only possibilities. The positions of the chords alternate: the ii chord is in A position, the V is in B, and the I is in A. Example 4-2 illustrates the progression with the ii chord in B position; notice that the voice leading is exactly the same.

Example 4-2 *The ii-V-I Progression, B-A-B Positions*

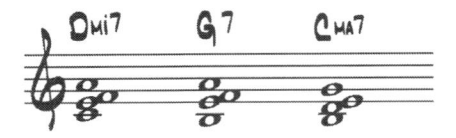

```
Dmi7       G7        Cma7
```

A great advantage to studying and practicing the ii-V-I progression is that harmonic rules are easily seen and digested (as Example 4-1 illustrates). This ubiquitous progression also provides an opportunity to explore various substitutions, options regarding the V chord, the progression in minor, and the use of borrowed harmony. Example 4-3 illustrates the progression in C minor. In this case, the chord tone substitutes are included in the symbols, which is common in minor. (But again, these are not the only possibilities, as will be discussed below).

Example 4-3 *The ii-V-I Progression in Minor, A-B-A Positions*

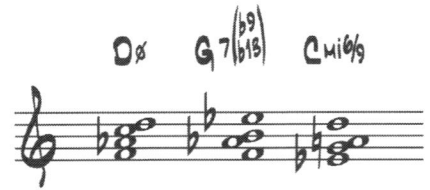

```
Dø      G7(b9/b13)    Cmi6/9
```

Advanced Harmonic Progression: Four-Way Close Voicings

Alternative Chord Tone Substitutions Available in Minor

Example 4-4 includes chord tone substitutions that differ slightly from what is presented in Example 4-3. Note that in the example above, there is no ninth in the ii chord (the D half diminished). In the chord note substitution chart in Example 3-2, a major ninth is shown as a possible alteration for a half-diminished chord (labeled as a minor seven/flat five, which is equivalent to a half-diminished chord). Since the major ninth of the D half diminished chord is an E natural, it is the major third of the key of C minor, and could present a problem. However, because of the color provided by the melodic minor modes (you may need to review this topic in your jazz theory textbooks), there is a melodic minor mode that generates a major ninth on a half-diminished chord – the locrian sharp two mode (the sixth melodic minor mode). Further, the V chord in Example 4-3 contains chord tones that have been generated from the harmonic minor scale – namely, the E♭ and A♭. However, there is the possibility of raising the ninth rather than lowering it (an A♯ rather than A♭); this again is derived from a melodic minor mode – the super locrian (also known as *altered* and is the seventh melodic minor mode*)* in this case. Example 4-4 illustrates the ii-V-I in minor, using B-A-B positions, and with alternative chord tone substitutions.

Example 4-4 *The ii-V-I Progression in Minor, B-A-B Positions*

Adding a Secondary Dominant – Turning Around the ii-V-I

A useful drill in mastering the ii-V-I progression is to create a repeating pattern. By inserting a secondary dominant – a V/ii – following the I chord, the progression will repeat, as follows:

Example 4-5 *The ii-V-I-V/ii Progression in Major, Both Positions*

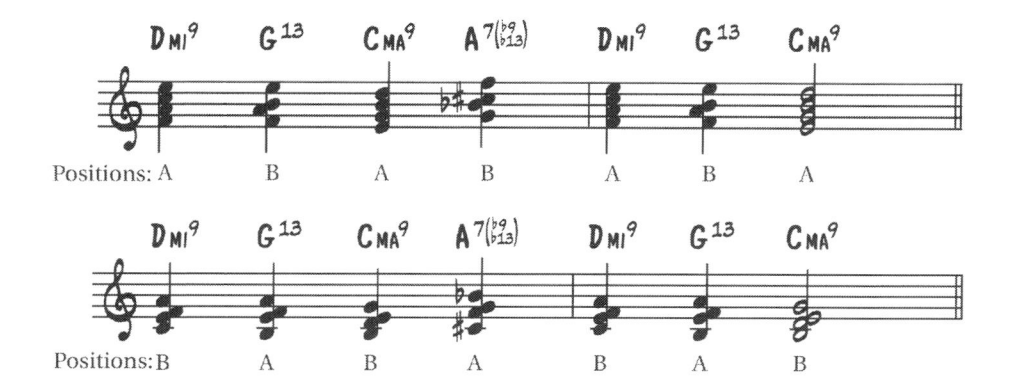

44 Part I: Voicings and Harmonic Progression

Example 4-6 The ii-V-i-V/ii Progression in Minor, Both Positions

[Musical notation showing the progression with chord symbols: Dø, G7(♭9,♭13), Cmi6/9, A7(♭9,♭13), Dø, G7(♭9,♭13), Cmi6/9 across two lines, with Positions labeled A and B alternating]

Secondary dominants are ubiquitous chords in jazz (and common-practice classical) harmony. The progression above offers an opportunity to explore various options regarding this important chord. Note the chord tone subs used for the V/ii chord. This chord is functioning in the key of D minor, since that's its role in the progression – to lead to the D minor chord. It is in B position because it is leading to an A position D minor chord, thus following proper voicing leading of alternating positions. Since the A7 is directed toward a minor chord, the chord tone substitutes – the B♭ (flatted ninth) and F (the flatted thirteenth) should be those generated by the D harmonic minor scale. Again, this is not the only possibility – super locrian-generated substitutes (like the sharped nine) are also common.

The following exercises drill the ii-V-I-V/ii-ii-V-I progression, in major and minor, and in the two positions described above.

Exercise 4-1: ii-V-I-V/ii Progression: Two Positions, All Major and Minor Keys

Practice and memorize the progression in every key. Note that key signatures are used in this exercise (unlike in the examples above). Play the chords in the right hand and the roots in the left; then practice the chords in the left hand while the right hand rests.

Advanced Harmonic Progression: Four-Way Close Voicings

Chord Positions: A-B-A-B-A-B-A

46 Part I: Voicings and Harmonic Progression

Chord Positions: B-A-B-A-B-A-B

Advanced Harmonic Progression: 47
Four-Way Close Voicings

Placing the Progression Within A Musical Context

As was illustrated in Chapter 3, it is useful to not only practice voicings and progressions in all keys, one after another (usually using the circle of fourths), it is also helpful to 'jam', where one key is played in a musical setting (as in a 'jam session'). Example 4-7 illustrates this idea. The bossa nova groove used in Examples 3-3 and 3-4 is again seen here. Note that the progression begins with a ii-V motion repeated three times; this actually could go on for much longer before moving to the I and V/ii chords. Also, various positions and rhythms could be used as demonstrated in Example 3-4.

Example 4-7 "Jam Session" Repetitive Progression: the ii-V-I-V/ii - Musical Context

Exercise 4-2: "Jam Session" Repetitive Progression: the ii-V-I-V/ii

Play the example above and remain in one key for as long as you like. The object is to get to the point where you don't have to think about the chord tones – you're just making music. Invert the progression as well, beginning with an 'A' position ii chord.

48 Part I: Voicings and Harmonic Progression

As a culminating exercise in four-way close position, the following progression moves to the relative minor of each key. A IV chord is used as a transitional chord. These are notated in only C and A minor, beginning with the ii chord in A position, and then in B position.

Example 4-8 ii-V-I – *Major and Relative Minor – Four-way Close*

> **Exercise 4-3: ii-V-I – Major and Relative Minor**
>
> Practice and memorize the progression displayed in Example 4-8 in every key. Play the chords in the right hand and the roots in the left; then practice the chords in the left hand while the right hand rests.

GLT I and II – Four-Way Close Voicings

The *Guided Learning Tunes* are notated below using four-way close voicings in the left hand. This is different from Example 3-5 because the melody is not being harmonized here – the chords are serving as an accompaniment part. They therefore are in either A or B voicing, and flow with proper voice leading. The melodies have been transposed up an octave to avoid the hands colliding (but it certainly could be played in the original octave, as long as the hands stay out each other's way). These same voicings could also be used in the right hand when accompanying someone playing the melody. In that case, you would likely play some sort of bass line in the left hand. Specific accompaniment patterns will be discussed in Part II; these examples focus on the proper voicings.

Advanced Harmonic Progression: 49
Four-Way Close Voicings

Example 4-9 *GLT I with Four-Way Close Voicings, Left Hand*

50   Part I: Voicings and Harmonic Progression

Example 4-10 GLT II with Four-Way Close Voicings, Left Hand

Close Position Progressions – Beyond the Four-Note Structure

Chapter 3 concludes with section about adding clusters within close structures. Example 4-11 illustrates a ii-V-I progression in C major, beginning with the ii chord in A position, and then beginning in B position. Note the color clusters throughout the example. As addressed in Chapter 3, transposing these is not always practical, as the clusters are sometimes performed with the thumb depressing two adjacent tones.

Example 4-11 Close Position Progression with Clusters

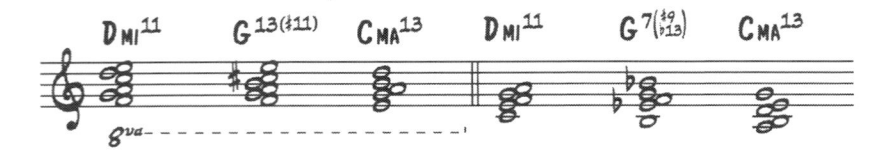

Advanced Harmonic Progression: Four-Way Close Voicings

Exercise 4-4: ii-V-I – Close Position with Clusters

Practice and memorize the progression displayed in Example 4-11 in various keys. The key will determine which clusters can be employed (because of the combination of white and black keys). Play the chords in the right hand, and the roots in the left; then practice the chords in the left hand while the right hand rests.

5

Open Position Voicings

The term *open,* when referring to a voicing, simply means that the voicing spans an interval greater than an octave. Open position voicings are identified as drop-2, drop-3 (less common), and drop-2/4 (which will be introduced in the quartal harmony section below). Tonal clusters are also common in open position voicings.

Drop-2

A drop-2 voicing is created by simply dropping the second highest voice of a four-way close tertian structure down an octave to the bottom of the chord. It is by far the most frequently used open position. This type of voicing allows the listener to hear the individual parts of the chord much more clearly than in a close voicing. It is also an effective two-handed voicing approach. Example 5-1 illustrates the simple process of converting a four-way close voicing into drop-2:

Example 5-1 *Converting Four-Way Close into Drop-2*

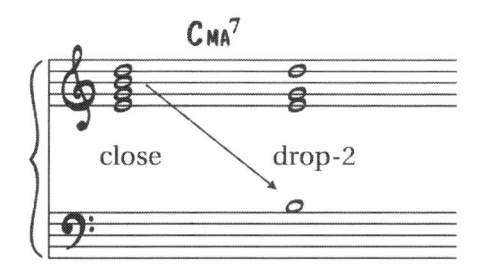

Notice that the outer voices form a tenth. Because the outer voices are so prevalent in an open voicing, they should form a consonant interval. This can affect chord tone substitution choices, as is seen in Example 5-2.

Example 5-2 *Drop-2 Illustration with Consonant Outer Voice Interval*

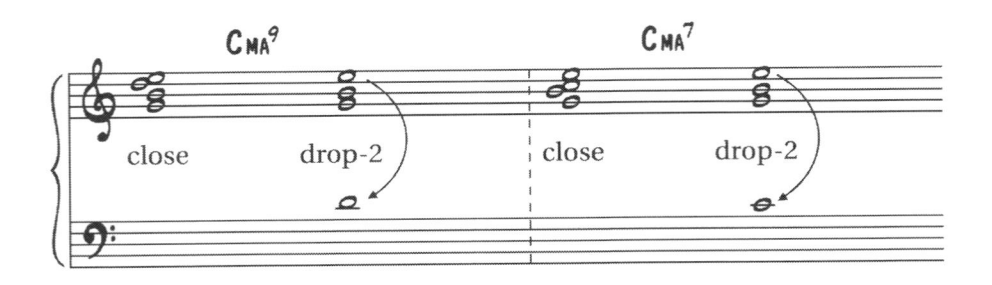

In the first measure, a ninth has been substituted for the root, and it is the second voice from the top. When that voice is dropped, a ninth is formed between the outer voices, which sounds awkward. The second measure corrects the problem by using the root of the chord, rather than a ninth, thereby creating a tenth in the outer voices.

Exercise 5-1 mirrors Exercise 3-1, where four-way close voicings are to be practiced around the circle of fourths. Again, only major, dominant, and minor sevenths are notated. While there are no 'A' and 'B' labels (since the bottom note has changed), it is still useful to think of them in that way. If the right hand thumb is playing the third, than an 'A' position chord is being played; if the thumb is playing the seventh, than a 'B' position chord is being played.

> **Exercise 5-1:** Drop-2 Voicings: Major, Dominant, and Minor Sevenths – Circle of Fourths
>
> Practice the chords below. Be aware of each and every chord tone as you play the exercise. Playing a root with left hand pinky finger is recommended so that each chord quality is heard clearly.

Open Position Voicings

A position:

(musical notation: Cma7, Fma7, B♭ma7, E♭ma7, A♭ma7, D♭ma7, F#ma7, Bma7, Ema7, Ama7, Dma7, Gma7)
— 7 moved down an octave

(musical notation: C7, F7, B♭7, E♭7, A♭7, D♭7, F#7, B7, E7, A7, D7, G7)
— 9 subs for root, 13 subs for 5

(musical notation: Cmi7, Fmi7, B♭mi7, E♭mi7, A♭mi7, D♭mi7, F#mi7, Bmi7, Emi7, Ami7, Dmi7, Gmi7)

B position:

(musical notation: Cma7, Fma7, B♭ma7, E♭ma7, A♭ma7, D♭ma7, F#ma7, Bma7, Ema7, Ama7, Dma7, Gma7)
— 3 moves down an octave

(musical notation: C7, F7, B♭7, E♭7, A♭7, D♭7, F#7, B7, E7, A7, D7, G7)
— 9 subs for root, no sub for 5 (as in Exercise 3-1)

(musical notation: Cmi7, Fmi7, B♭mi7, E♭mi7, A♭mi7, D♭mi7, F#mi7, Bmi7, Emi7, Ami7, Dmi7, Gmi7)

Example 5-3 illustrates *Guided Learning Tune I* using drop-2 voicings. This version is based upon the four-way close harmonization shown in Example 3-5. Note that the left hand is now playing a chord tone (the dropped voice) rather than the bass voice. Also notice that the outer voicings form tenths in almost all cases. There are two locations where the left-hand part duplicates the melody an octave lower – on the D half diminished chord in measure 4 and on the Cmi7 in measure 5. The range of the melody is the determining factor in those cases.

56 Part I: Voicings and Harmonic Progression

Example 5-3 *GLT I with Drop-2 Voicings Harmonizing the Melody*

Quartal Structures

Tertian harmony, as we saw in Chapter 1, refers to building chords by stacking in thirds. While this is the most common method of building chords, it is not the only way. Chords can be constructed by stacking seconds ("secundal"), fourths ("quartal"), and fifths ("quintal"). The use of fourths in jazz became prevalent during the 1960s in the music of artists such as McCoy Tyner, Miles Davis, Joe Henderson and many others. You'll find that if you apply quartal harmony properly, your playing will take on a more spacious, hip sound. As we explore quartal harmony in this section, we'll build on the concepts introduced in the previous chapters – especially the concept of open voicing structures.

Quartal voicings are constructed with perfect fourths, except in the case of the dominant seventh in which the bottom interval is a tritone. These are normally conceived of as five note structures, although they can also be played with four or three notes. There are a couple of interesting points about quartal harmony which we will discuss shortly:

1. Quartal voicings can be thought of as drop-2/4 open voicings derived from a tertian structure.

2. Depending on what the root is, the same stack of fourths can form several different chords.

Open Position Voicings   57

Quartal Harmony = Drop-2/4

As mentioned above, drop-2/4 voicings can be voiced as quartal voicings. This way of thinking about drop-2/4 is actually simpler then thinking about lowering the second and fourth notes from the top of a chord. The conversion from close position to drop-2/4 is illustrated in Example 5-4.

The chord on the left of Example 5-4 is a five note C major structure in close position that contains, from the top down, the root, sixth, fifth, third, and ninth. (Five part chords do not follow the chord tone substitution roles discussed earlier, as there is an additional tone). The chord structure on the right has the same notes but is voiced with a drop-2/4 voicings. The second and fourth notes from the top (the A and E) have been dropped an octave resulting in a chord built entirely of perfect fourths.

Example 5-4 *Quartal Structure Derived from Drop-2/4*

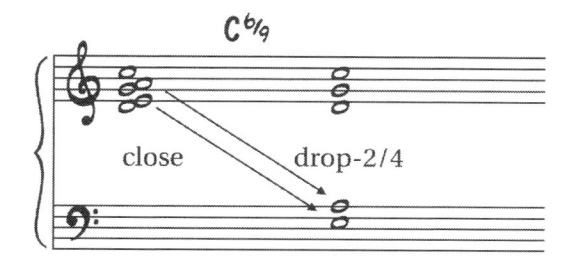

Quartal structures also have the added benefit of flexibility. The same five-note structure can actually be thought of as several chords. Pianists and arrangers know instinctively what chord tone they are harmonizing (that is, the top tone), and apply the appropriate quartal voicing. Example 5-5 illustrates the concept – the quartal structure from Example 5-4 can be used as a C, F, or A minor.

Example 5-5 *Quartal Structures With Different Roots*

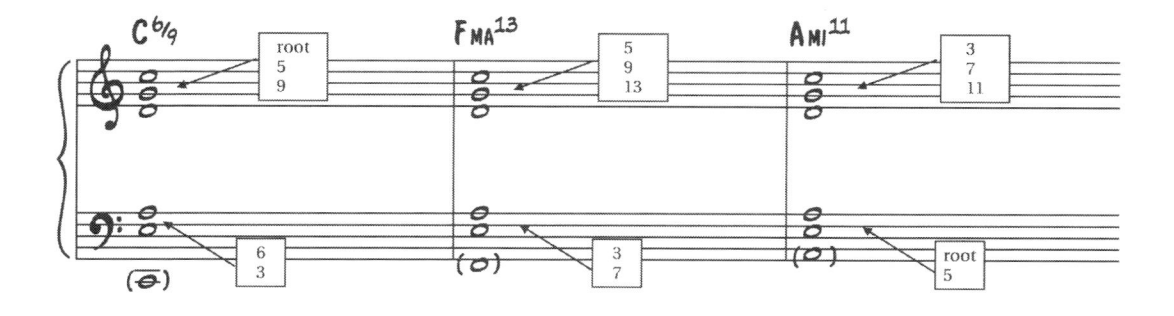

58 Part I: Voicings and Harmonic Progression

> ### Exercise 5-2: Quartal Chord Structures – Circle of Fourths
>
> Practice the following chords around the circle of fourths. Note that chord symbols are not included as these structures can form various chords, as explained above.

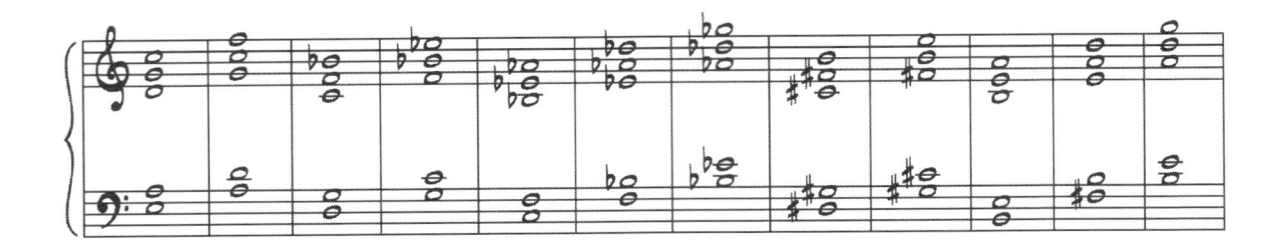

Diatonic Quartal Structures

　　　Quartal structures can be constructed on every note of a major scale. When constructed of five notes, as described above, a pattern emerges, where perfect fourth stacks occur when the root, fourth, or fifth of the scale are on top of the chord. Example 5-6 illustrates quartal structures that occur in the key of C. These same structures could be used in the diatonic modes derived from C major (D dorian, E phrygian, etc). These voicings, therefore, are useful when comping in a modal setting within a static harmony.

Example 5-6 Quartal Structures in the Key of C (and its related modes)

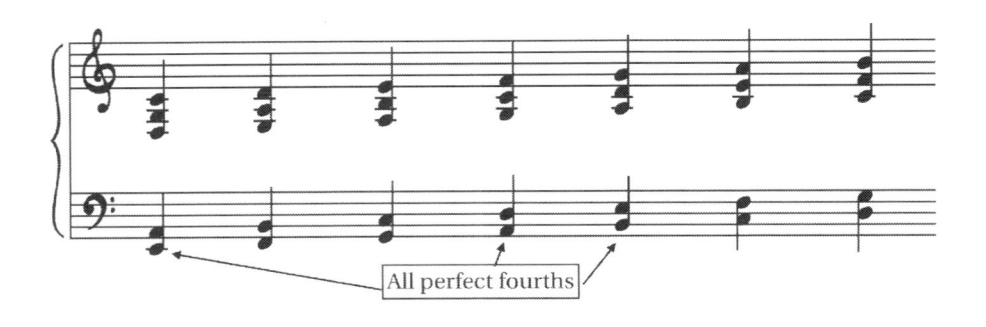

All perfect fourths

> ### Exercise 5-3: Modal Planing
>
> Practice Example 5-6 in all keys.

Quartal Structures as Dominants

So far we have only discussed major and minor quartal voicings. It is possible to use quartal voicings for dominant chords as well, but in order to do so the bottom interval of the voicing must be altered. By converting the bottom interval into a tritone (diminished fifth or augmented fourth) the chord becomes a bright sounding dominant seventh.

Example 5-7 illustrates the conversion of major or minor quartal structures into dominant chords. They should be practiced in the same manner as the quartal structures notated in Exercise 5-2; simply change the bottom interval into a tritone interval.

Example 5-7 *Dominant Quartal Structures*

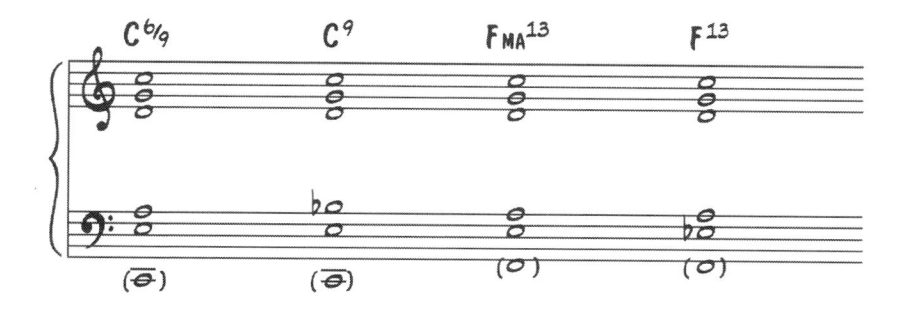

Exercise 5-4: Dominant Quartal Structures

Practice the dominant chords displayed in Example 5-7 in all keys.

Finally – there will be a discussion of three note voicings in Chapter 7; at that point, quartal voicings will be re-visited as three-note structures, useful as intense-sounding single hand voicings.

So What Voicings

So What voicings, named for the Miles Davis composition, are similar to the quartal voicings discussed above, but this structure is brightened by the presence of a major third interval on top of the chord. This voicing has the same properties as the quartal chords – it is a drop-2/4 voicing and is transposable. These are illustrated below.

60 Part I: Voicings and Harmonic Progression

Example 5-8 So What Voicings with Different Roots

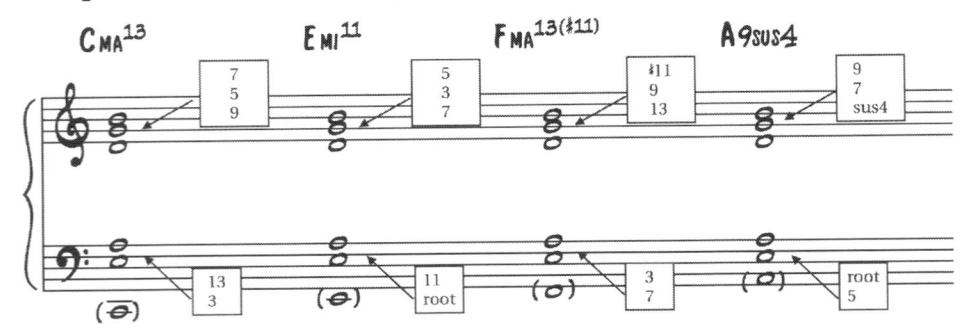

Exercise 5-5: *So What* Voicing Structures

Practice the following chords around the circle of fourths. Note that chord symbols are not included as these structures can be various chords, as explained above.

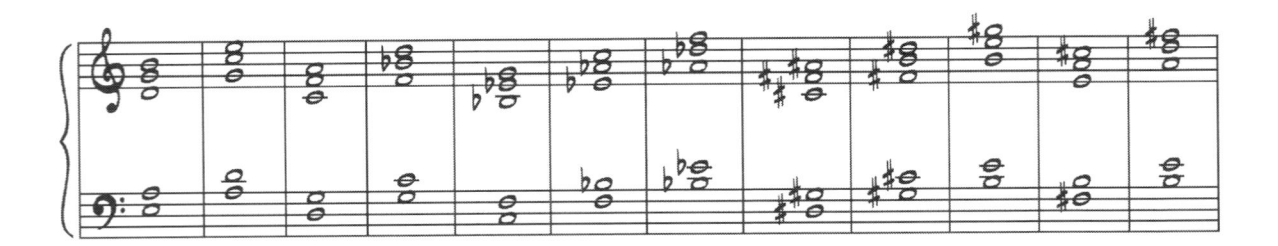

Modal Planing with Quartal Harmony

Quartal structures provide a useful tool when harmonizing within a modal environment. Quartal chords, in three, four, or five notes, can shift either diatonically (as in Example 5-6, within the 'mode of the moment') or chromatically, which creates opportunities to create tension and release. McCoy Tyner is the most well-known proponent of this type of playing. He often included a low perfect fifth to provide a foundation.

Example 5-9 illustrates *Guided Learning Tune II* played with quartal structures. While this type of playing is often used in a static modal situation, (i.e. a long span of a single mode), it also can an effective method for the blues. In order to best demonstrate this approach, the chord symbols have been simplified, so that a more modal sound can be achieved.

Example 5-9 *GLT II with Modal Planing*

Example 5-9 above uses the F mixolydian mode for the basic structure, as many of the quartal chords are comprised of those tones. Note the chromatic planing however, as well as the triadic structure in measure four, beat three. There are also foundational low fifths on the I, IV, and V chords at important structural points of the blues progression.

Slash Chords

Because pianists play with two hands, we often are viewing and feeling chords as two entities – something in the right hand and something in the left. For example, by playing an E minor triad in the right hand – E, G, B – and a C in the left, we are actually playing a Cma7 chord.

62 Part I: Voicings and Harmonic Progression

There is a system for this dual approach to chord playing known as *slash chord notation.* A slash chord is a symbol that indicates a bass note or chord (often just the root and seventh) to be played by the left hand with a chord, often a second inversion triad, to be played in the right. These are labeled with the right-hand chord on the left of a slash; the bass note or chord is on the right. They are useful in expressing a complicated chord structure in a simple way, and are often, but not always, dominant chords. For example, a C7 with a raised ninth and lowered thirteenth would result in a complicated chord symbol. But when notated as an A♭/C7 chord, it is quite simple. Example 5-10 includes six common slash chord structures. Note that the first two have the same upper triad, with bass notes separated by a tritone; the same is true of the third and fourth chords. This demonstrates the use of tritone substitution.

Example 5-10 Common Slash Chords

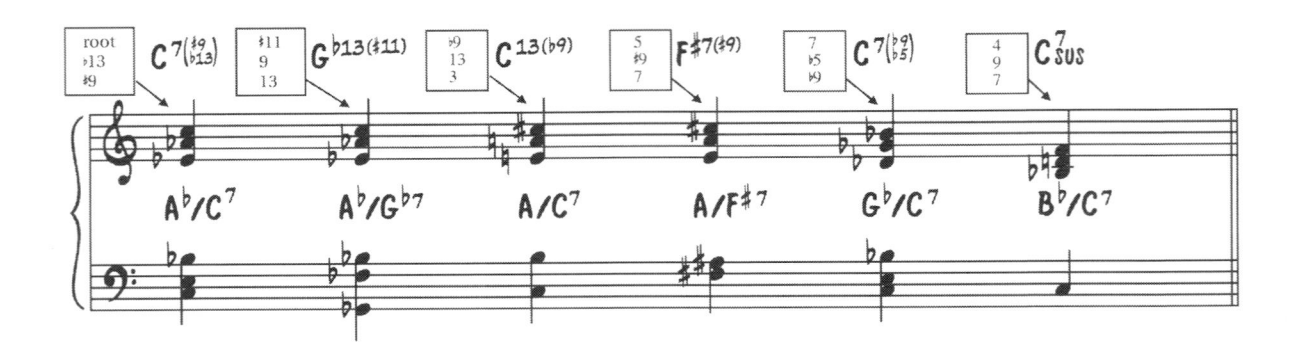

The example above shows the slash chord symbol between the staves and the more complicated single symbol above the treble staff. The chord tones supplied by the upper triad symbol are listed in the boxes to the left of the chord symbol. Like the quartal and *So What* voicings, the A♭/C7 and A♭/G♭7 slash chords are five-note structures (not including the roots). The A/C7 and G♭/C7 are four-note chords (not including the root). (The G♭/C7 includes a doubled seventh, played by the left hand thumb). Notice that the enharmonic spelling is flexible when using these voicings. In the A♭/C7, the E♭ in the treble staff appears to be a minor third, but since there is a major third in the chord (in the bass clef), it is an enharmonically misspelled raised ninth (♯9). The reason for the E♭ rather than a D♯ is that the upper triad is an A♭ chord, which of course contains an E♭.

Slash chord notation has another important role; it is helpful in creating smoother bass lines by indicating inversions (i.e., C – C/E – F – G). In this case, only a letter name will be indicated for the bass note, as the C/E is a first inversion C chord, leading to the F.

Open Position Voicings

Exercise 5-6: Slash Chord Voicing Structures

Practice the following chords around the circle of fourths.

Dominant #9, b13 & Dominant 13, #11 Chords

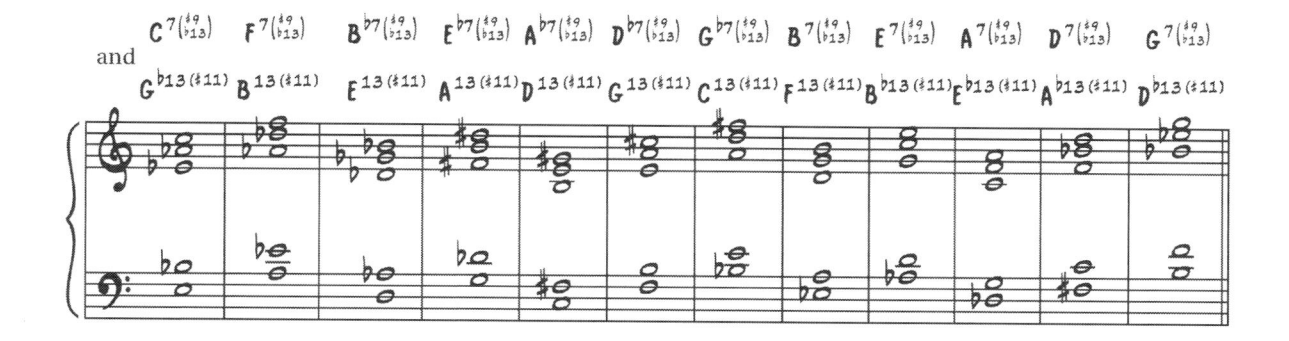

Dominant 13/b9 & Dominant #9 Chords

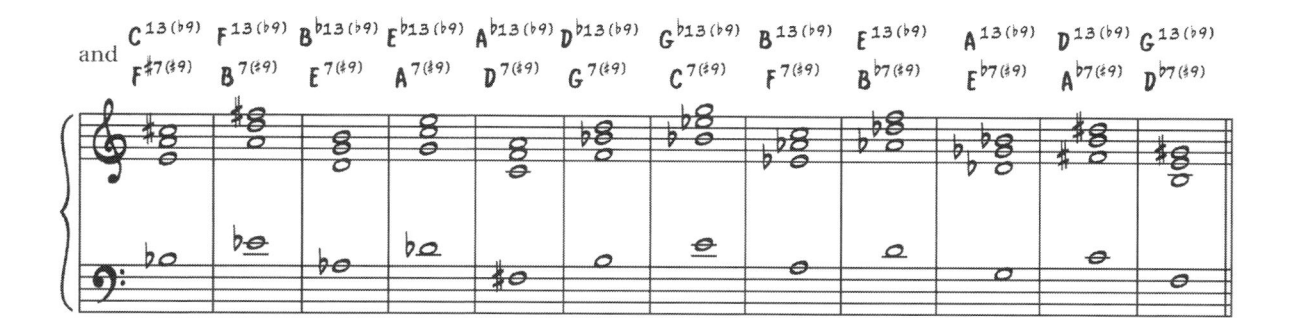

Dominant b9, b5 Chords

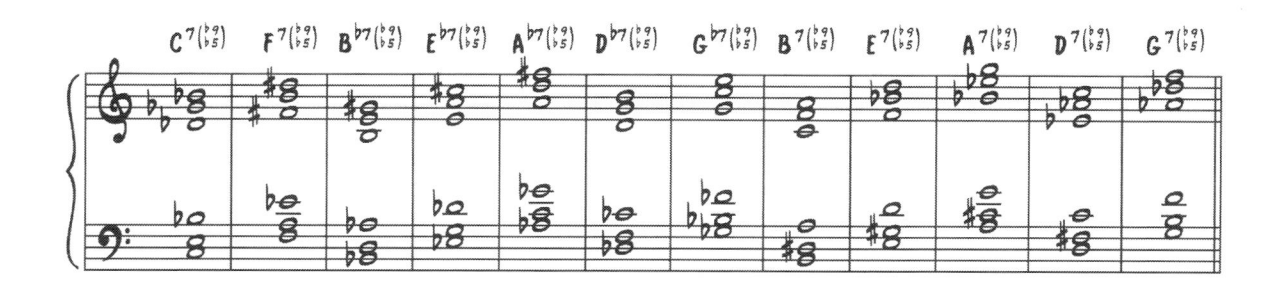

64 Part I: Voicings and Harmonic Progression

Dominant Suspended 4 Chords

Open Position Voicings With Tonal Clusters

Chapters 3 and 4 conclude with a section describing close position voicings – those that fall within an octave – but with clusters. We can add a layer of color to open position voicings as well, by including clusters, often in the middle of the chord. As with any chord voicing and progression, it is critical to understand the harmonic underpinning at the moment as you add tones to form clusters. That being said, those chords are often used to move in and out of the harmony, as they have a non-functional quality to them. Color is the name of the game here.

Since we have eight fingers and two thumbs, we can play ten, or ever more notes at the same time, because the thumbs can press down two notes, and are therefore very useful in creating clusters. Example 5-11 illustrates a ten(!) note Cma13 voicing. In this case, the left hand plays the D and E in the bass clef; the right hand thumb plays the G and A. Note that this voicing is constructed of a G major pentatonic scale above a C bass note.

Example 5-11 Open Voicing With Clusters

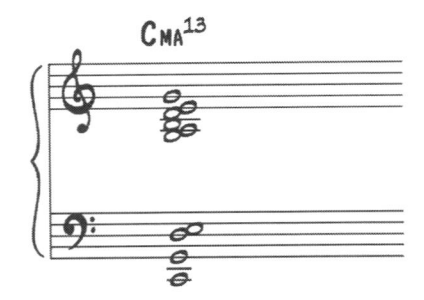

It is stated in Chapter 3 that understanding the mode operating at a given moment is very helpful in determining the extra tones when adding clusters. The voicing in Example 5-11 obviously would be occurring in C major (or ionian), or G major (or C lydian). This particular chord is quite simple to play because it is constructed of only white notes, and each thumb can depress two notes. (The G and A in the right hand thumb; the D and E in the left hand thumb). However, voicings that include black notes, offer other possibilities of arranging our fingers and playing clusters. The next example illustrates several chords that contain color and tension, with a mix of white and black notes. Some of the chords would need to be rolled, or played with the outer voices first, following by the inner voices. (This technique is explored in Chapter 9 as an accompaniment method). Finally, visualizing chords with an hour-glass shape is a useful image, where inner clusters (often played with the thumbs) are paired with larger interval spans on the top and bottom of the structure.

Example 5-12 Open Voicing With Clusters – Various

GLT I is presented in Example 5-13 (below Exercise 5-7, where you are instructed to experiment with open chords with clusters). The example illustrates accompanying chords using clusters, as explained in Chapters 3, 4, and this chapter. These complex chords add colorful tensions not available in four-way close or open positions. Again, their conception is based on color rather than a systematic substitution process – although that process is still in play – just adjusted for a different effect. The original chords are notated above the melody; the full chord symbols of the chords with clusters are notated above the grand staff.

Exercise 5-7: Open Position Voicings with Clusters

Experiment with open position voicings with added clusters. Listen carefully for the effect being created. Begin with the voicings illustrated in Examples 5-11 and 5-12.

66 Part I: Voicings and Harmonic Progression

Example 5-13 GLT I with Cluster Voicings

6
Open Position Harmonic Motion

Drop-2 — ii-V-I-V/ii Motion

As was described in Chapter 5, drop-2 voicings are simply four-way close voicings with the second note from the top dropped an octave. The exercise below illustrates the ii-V-I-V/ii progression and includes the four chord tones, and also the root — so the left hand plays the roots plus the dropped voice. The following examples contain the same voice movement as seen in four-way close voicings, in Examples 4-5 and 4-6

Example 6-1 ii-V-I-V/ii Progression – Drop-2

Beginning with A Position:

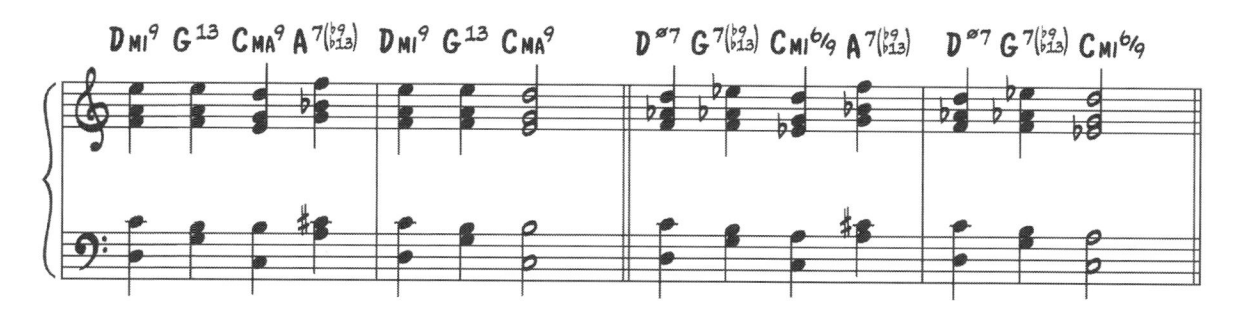

Beginning with B Position:

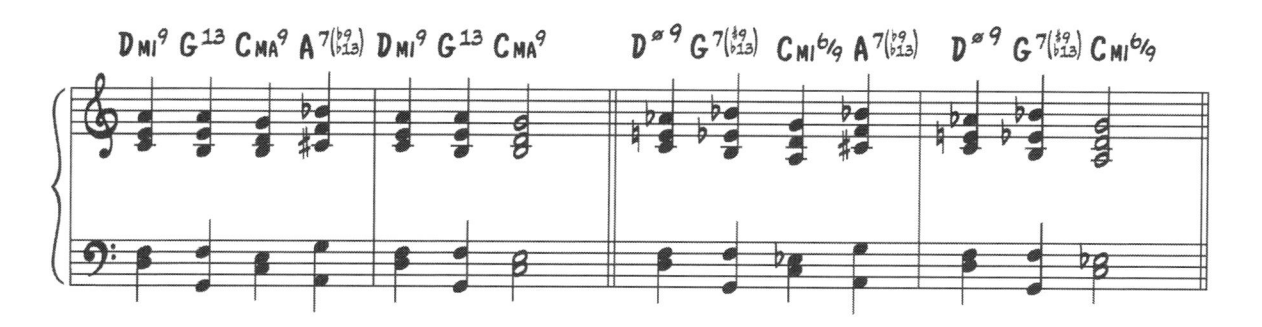

68 Part I: Voicings and Harmonic Progression

> ***Exercise 6-1:* ii-V-I-V/ii Progression – Drop-2**
>
> Practice and memorize the progression illustrated in Example 6-1 in every key. Do this by following Exercise 4-1 and dropping the second voice from the top into the left hand.

The same culminating exercise seen in Example 4-8, in four-way close, is presented below in drop-2 – in major and the relative minor. Again, these are notated in only C and A minor and are in both chord positions.

Example 6-2 ii-V-I – Major and Relative Minor – Drop-2

> ***Exercise 6-2:* ii-V-I – Major and Relative Minor**
>
> Practice and memorize the progression displayed in Example 6-2 in every key.

Quartal, *So What*, and Slash Chords – ii-V-I Motion

The examples below illustrate two ways to employ quartal, *So What*, and slash chords as ii-V-I's. There are many ways to go about this – these examples offer just a sample of how these structures can add color and tension to the progression. Because these are constructed differently than four-way close and drop-2, the voice-leading is a little different.

Example 6-3 So What, Slash Chord, Quartal ii-V-I

Example 6-3 begins with a *So What* voicing for the ii chord, a slash chord for the V chord (which is actually a dominant 13,♭9 chord) and a four voice quartal structure (not counting the root) for the I chord.

Example 6-4 Parallel So What ii-V-I Progression

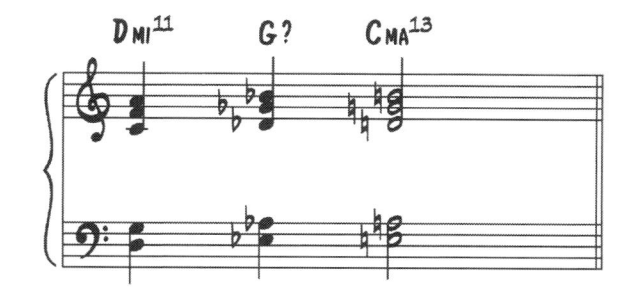

Example 6-4 is constructed of three *So What* chords ascending by half step. The resulting chord structures provide standard chord tones for the ii and the I, but the V chord is non-functional – hence the chord symbol "G?". The progression works well, however, since the momentum of the chromatic movement allows for the G chord to 'sound' correct.

Exercise 6-3: ii-V-I – *So What,* Quartal, Slash Chords

Practice and memorize the progression displayed in Examples 6-3 and 6-4 in every key.

70 Part I: Voicings and Harmonic Progression

GLT I and II – Quartal, So What, Slash Chord Comping

The final examples of this chapter illustrate comping versions of the *Guided Learning Tunes* using quartal, *So What*, and slash chords. The melody has been placed in a staff above the grand staff for reference. The comping rhythms match Examples 4-9 and 4-10 which demonstrate four-way close left hand voicings.

Example 6-5 *GLT I with Quartal, So What, and Slash Chord Voicings: Two-Hand Comping*

Open Position Harmonic Motion   71

Note the blend of the three voicing types. This is also an example of comping where the roots are included on the bottom of the left hand. The comping for *GLT II* below illustrates rootless voicings, and also features a blend of the three voicing types presented in this chapter.

Example 6-6 *GLT II with Quartal, So What, and Slash Chord Voicings: Two-Hand Comping*

7

Three-Part Voicings

Playing with three-part chords presents a unique challenge, but also offers alternative sounds that provide clarity and exciting **dissonance to chord** voicings. The challenge in using these voicings is that a chord tone must be **eliminated** from the basic four note structure. There are two considerations to keep in mind **when using three** note voicings: which chord tone will be eliminated and the type of chord structure.

Shell Voicings

Shell voicing is a common term used for three-note chords. The object is to include the third and seventh of a chord, and add one additional chord, such as the fifth or ninth.

Example 7-1 Shell Voicings

Quartal Voicings and Clusters

Often, two fourths are stacked one on top of the other, thereby forming a quartal structure. These chords can be inverted just like any other chord. Doing so creates interesting whole steps, either on top of the chord (x) or **on the** bottom (y). The inverted structures (x and y) form a simplified version of a cluster voicing.

74 Part I: Voicings and Harmonic Progression

Example 7-2 *Quartal and Cluster Voicings*

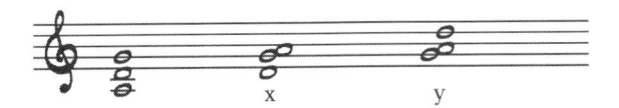

Three-note dominant seventh chords are often voiced with a perfect fourth over a tritone. These are extremely useful left hand voicings, with the potential of creating enormous tension and excitement. They often move parallel in and out of the harmony, creating 'outside' playing.

Example 7-3 *Dominant Shell Voicings*

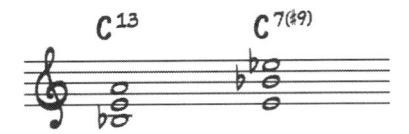

> ### Exercise 7-1: Three-Part Chords
>
> Practice and memorize the voicings displayed in Examples 7-1, 7-2, and 7-3 in every key. Play the chords in the right hand and the roots in the left; then practice the chords in the left hand while the right hand rests.

Three-Part Chords in a Progression

The ii-V-I-V/ii chord progression, when played with three-note voicings, offers a variety of choices. Example 7-4 illustrates several ways to voice the progression, including voicings seen in Examples 7-1, 7-2, and 7-3.

Example 7-4 The ii-V-I-V/ii Progression using Three-Part Chords

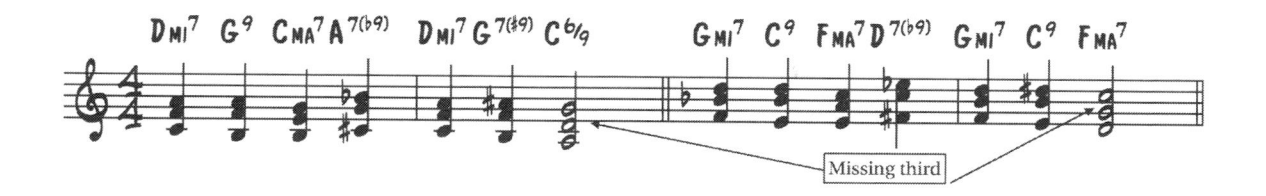

[Musical notation: Dmi7 G9 Cma7 A7(b9) Dmi7 G7(#9) C6/9 | Gmi7 C9 Fma7 D7(b9) Gmi7 C9 Fma7, with annotation "Missing third"]

> **Exercise 7-2:** The ii-V-I-V/ii using Three-Part Chords
>
> Practice and memorize the progression displayed in Example 7-4 in every key. Use the circle of fourths, up and down chromatically, or 'jam' in one key at a time before moving on to another key. Play the chords in the right hand and the roots in the left; then practice the chords in the left hand while the right hand rests.

Three-Part Left Hand Voicings

Guided Learning Tune II offers an excellent opportunity to hear and practice the potential of three-part chords. The predominance of dominant harmony in a blues works well with the stark nature of these voicings. Note the parallel motion in measures three and five. This is known as *side-slipping*. This example is similar to Example 5-9 where open position chords are illustrated.

76 Part I: Voicings and Harmonic Progression

Example 7-5 *GLT II with Three Note Voicings*

8

Re-harmonization Principles

This vast topic will be tackled as a way of an introduction to the process, offering two general methods for re-imagining jazz harmony. There are jazz piano books, and especially arranging and jazz theory sources, that tackle this topic with great detail. The purpose here is to offer some general suggestions, and use *Guided Learning Tune I* to illustrate some possibilities. Further reading and study, as well as transcribing, should be undertaken for a broader picture of this important concept.

A common technique for jazz pianists is to use a re-harmonized version of a jazz standard as an introduction, setting up the rest of the performance. These are often played rubato and have a rich harmonic structure. While there are many great examples to cite, check out two masters of this craft: Bill Evans and Keith Jarrett, as they harmonize standards from the great American songbook performing in their trio formats. Re-harmonization can be thought of in two ways: using <u>functional</u> harmony, or thinking primarily in terms of tone-color and effect – that is, <u>non-functional</u>. These methods are explored below.

Functional Re-Harmonization

Functional re-harmonization is at its essence a 'following of harmonic rules', where traditional methods are employed. For example, inserting secondary function, using tritone substitution, pedal points, and other methods that use harmonic-based tools are examples of functional re-harmonization. The methods listed below illustrate some of these possibilities – but the options are practically endless.

1. Diatonic chord substitution (for example, vi for I)

2. Use of secondary dominants and secondary ii-V motion

3. Tritone substitution and secondary tritone substitution

4. Modal borrowing (borrowing from the parallel minor)

5. Use of pedal points to create tension

78 Part I: Voicings and Harmonic Progression

Example 8-1 illustrates these concepts using *GLT I*.

Example 8-1 *Guided Learning Tune I: Functional Re-harmonization*

Note the use of tritone secondary function in measure one (the B7, substituting for an F7, is leading to the Bbmi7) and measure 2 (the Eb/A7 slash chord substitutes for the Eb7). The Gb7 is the sub-tonic of Ab, and the G7 is acting as a passing harmony to the new tonic of Ab. The Ami11 begins a circle progression leading to the Cmi7 in measure five. The Gb7 is a tritone substitute for a C7, which leads to the Fmi7. (Also note that the rhythm is slightly changed here). This chord, paired with the Bb7, is borrowed from C dorian. Finally, the progression ends with the *Ladybird* cadence – C – Eb – Ab – G.

Non-Functional Reharmonization

Ignoring traditional functional tendencies can be an effective method to create innovative re-harmonizations. There are even more possibilities for re-harmonization using this method, but the original flow of the standard being re-harmonized can be compromised if care is not taken – so don't take this too far! This type of re-harmonization involves alternative voicings, parallelism, and chord color as the methodology. The term "non-functional" means just what it says – the harmonic rules are essentially ignored. It may be useful to combine the two approaches – functional and non-functional - where a tune can be treated without regard to function, but then function can re-occur at certain structural points, such as cadences. Example 8-2 illustrates this concept, again with *GLT I*. Note that the tempo marking is now "ballad", and would likely be played in a rubato fashion.

Example 8-2 Guided Learning Tune I: Non-functional Re-harmonization

Example 8-2 relies on chromatic motion and some parallelism, especially in measure 4. The arrangement concludes with the same *Ladybird* cadence pattern as in the functional version above.

***Exercise 8-1:* Re-harmonization Techniques**

Practice the versions of *GLT I* seen in Examples 8-1 and 8-2. Pick some jazz standards and attempt some of these approaches, working with harmonic rules in a functional approach, and listen mostly for tonal color in a non-functional version.

Part II
Rhythm and Style

The second part of the book combines rhythmic principles with comping and style. Simple and effective comping patterns are presented, as well as discussions of specific styles. Swing, Latin, rock ballad, and funk are explored. Special techniques, such as bass-line construction, locked hands, block chord voicings, stride, and boogie-woogie are presented.

9

Comping

Rhythm and style are central elements of jazz. The 'time' aspect combines with harmony and melody to provide jazz's propulsive nature. Jazz appreciation textbooks typically begin with an introductory chapter that defines terms such as 'swing', 'feel', 'syncopation', and many others; these words and their definitions help to explain what occurs when jazz musicians collaborate. If needed, visit jazz appreciation books you may have in your collection (or visit the internet). This chapter will build upon general rhythmic principles and present specific stylistic and rhythm concepts for jazz pianists. The examples illustrated are merely the tip of the iceberg in terms of comping patterns – it's a limitless topic. But these examples should provide some background for further study and practice.

Fundamentally, there are only three ways that a chord structure can be played by the hand of a jazz pianist: 1) all of the notes can be sounded together; 2) the chord tones can be played separately, as in an arpeggio; 3) the fingers can play most of the notes of the chord with the thumb striking one note. Keep these three ways of playing in mind as we move forward in this chapter.

Swing Comping

Jazz pianists spend an enormous amount of time accompanying, otherwise known as "comping". Even when a pianist is performing as a soloist, she is likely comping with the left hand. When playing in ensembles, the pianist is obviously backing up other musicians as melodies and solos are performed. Jeb Patton, in his excellent two volume text, *An Approach to Comping*[1], presents two basic comping patterns as follows:

---
[1] Jeb Patton, *An Approach to Comping: The Essentials, A Guide to Jazz Accompanying*. (Petaluma, CA: Sher Music, 2013), 14-19.

86 Part II: Rhythm and Style

1. a. Charleston (based upon the dance made popular in the 1920s)

b. Displaced Charleston (shifting the pattern over one eighth note)

2. Bebop scat phrase: "Ooh bop sh'bam", where the 'sh' is ghosted (i.e., implied more than sounded)

OOH   BOP   SH' BAM   OOH   BOP   SH'   BAM

   The example below illustrates these three comping rhythms using *GLT II*. Note that the melody is placed in the right hand, and the rhythms are played by the comping left hand.
   These comping patterns could also be played by the right hand with a left-hand bass line if accompanying a melody instrument; or these could be played in two handed voicings if playing in an ensemble with melody instruments and a bassist. The voicings are four-way close.

Example 9-1 Comping Patterns on GLT II

Latin Comping

The music of Latin American and Cuba is beyond the scope of this book, as it is an enormous and important topic. However, a few exercises are offered below as a means to get started with this complex and exciting music, and can get you through many gigging situations. A straight-eighth rhythmic feel is most common.

88   Part II: Rhythm and Style

Bossa Nova

A simple and very common Latin rhythm is the *bossa nova,* which originated in Brazil. Often on the bandstand, when someone calls for a Latin tune, a bossa nova is the go-to choice. Tunes such as *Girl From Ipanema, Desifinado,* and *Triste* are well-known bossa novas, and all are composed by Carlos Antonio Jobim. This bass line was first introduced in the text in Chapter 3, where four-way close voicings are to be performed in a musical setting.

Example 9-2 Bossa Nova Comping

Example 9-2 demonstrates a simple i-IV dorian *vamp*– a repeating series of a few chords. The example includes the bass line in the left hand. If one were playing this with a bassist, two handed voicings (drop-2, etc) could be used with the right-hand rhythm.

The Montuno

In discussing Latin playing, we are provided with an opportunity to introduce the common approach mentioned above, whereby a chord is separated between the fingers sounding several notes from the thumb, which plays just one. This is known as a "thumb-line" comping pattern. This pattern is used when creating a *montuno*. The montuno is a foundation for Cuban music, and is extremely flexible and varied. It is based upon the *clave*, which is an arrangement of rhythms spanning two measures. This is an enormous topic and further study is recommended. The examples below offer only a glance into this fantastic music.

Example 9-3 Montuno Over a C minor chord

Example 9-4 Montuno in Major and Relative Minor

Example 9-5 Montuno in Major and Relative Minor

As with the bossa nova, Examples 9-3, 9-4, and 9-5 include the bass line in the left hand. Note the placement of the bass notes on the fourth beats of each measure, rather than on the 'and of four' as seen in the bossa nova. If one were playing this with a bassist, the right hand could be doubled by the left, with the right hand moving up an octave.

Rock Ballad Comping

A common 'popular' piano comping pattern is similar to the Latin examples presented above. This type of playing is often heard as a 'rock ballad' type of song and is notated in Example 9-6.

90 Part II: Rhythm and Style

Example 9-6 Rock Ballad Comping

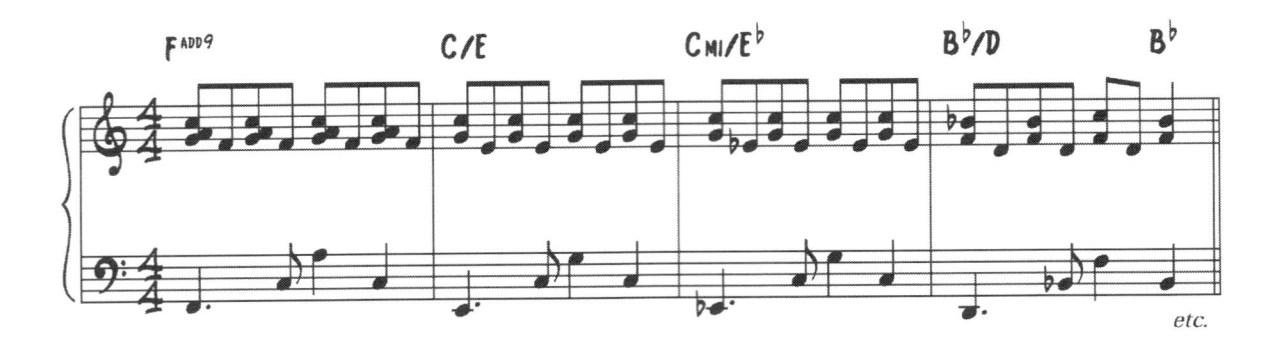

Note the bottom note of the chord in the right hand. It would be played by the thumb, as was described above. This example also includes an 'add 9' chord, where only the ninth (and not the seventh) is added to a triad. Finally, note the broken chord pattern in the left hand. This idea will be expanded to both hands in the next example.

Broken Chord Comping

Arpeggiating harmonic structures is a technique that is common in many types of music – certainly, and most fundamentally, in the classical tradition. The example below illustrates *GLT I* if played as a ballad; the melody would be assumed to be played by another instrument, as the accompaniment is spread throughout the grand staff. Note that the left hand is sounding the root, fifth, and tenth. This is a very common left hand foundation. The eighth notes would be played straight – even if the melody is played with a slight swing.

Example 9-7 Guided Learning Tune I – Ballad Accompaniment

Comping With Large Chords

One of the challenges for musicians performing as individuals, as well as ensembles, is balance among the melody, harmony, and bass notes. Chords with a large span complicates this task for pianists. A simple solution is one that not only helps in the playing of a large voicing, but also improves the balance. Example 9-8 illustrates the first three measures of *GLT I*, where wide chords are used as an accompaniment. Note that the outer voices sound together and the inner voices follow. This tends to balance the top of the chord (which even in an accompaniment is heard as a form of a melodic line) and the bass notes – which means they will be clearly heard.

92   Part II: Rhythm and Style

Example 9-8 Comping With Large Chords

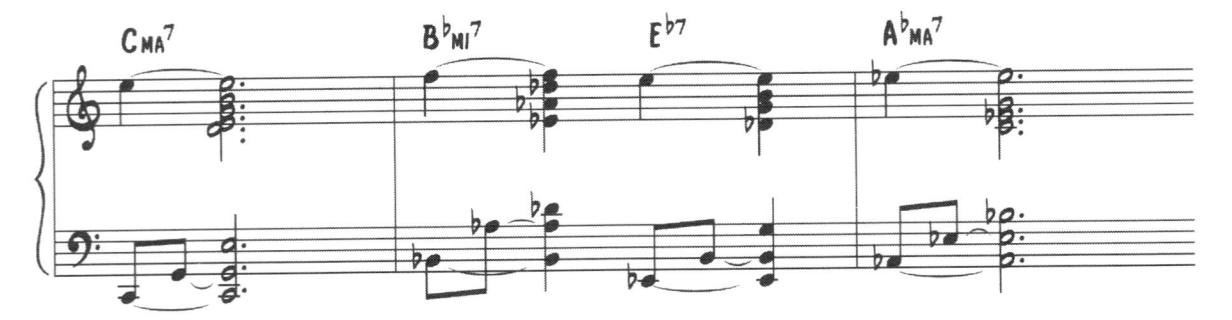

Funk Comping

Hand independence is vital in all piano-playing – but with funk playing it is critical. This style of music is highly syncopated, often emphasizing a sixteenth note feel. The example below offers a pattern that works well over a dominant seventh falling fifth vamp. In this example, the left hand would likely play these figures, even in the presence of a bass player.

Example 9-9 Funk Comping

Exercise 9-1: Comping

Practice the examples in this chapter and employ these techniques to jazz standards.

10
Special Techniques

The piano's flexibility, range, harmonic possibilities, and power make it an excellent instrument to feature special techniques. Classical music – especially piano music since 1950 – has included all types of special effects, including changing the piano physically (tacks on the hammers for example), strumming the strings, etc. For jazz pianists, techniques often are meant to resemble a larger ensemble. As is mentioned in the preface, Jelly Roll Morton often 'thought like a band' when he played the piano.

Bass Lines

With that in mind, the first special technique discussed in this chapter will be the playing of bass lines – that is, imitating an upright bass. Bassists normally play in either 'two' or 'four' when playing swing music. The focus will be on swing, since the Latin discussion in Chapter 9 involved the left hand playing bass lines and was discussed at that time. The examples below provide a framework for creating bass lines – but the possibilities are endless.

Bass Lines in "Two"

When a bassist (or a pianist's left hand) plays in 'two', the melody is normally being played, prior to the solos. This is a very advanced technique, and is difficult if not impossible to notate accurately. The feel and interpretation is the key here. It is essentially a half note rhythm (hence playing in 'two' – two bass notes per measure), but a bassist will normally add subtle grace notes. Example 10-1 illustrates a bass line in a 'two' feel over a ii-V-I-V/ii progression.

Example 10-1 Bass Line in a "Two" Feel

94   Part II: Rhythm and Style

Example 10-2 illustrates a 'two' feel using *Guided Learning Tune II*. The melody is placed in a staff above the piano part. You'll notice that there are occasional walking bass (playing in 'four') measures.

Example 10-2 *Guided Learning Tune II - Bass Line in "Two"*

Bass Lines in "Four"

Creating bass lines in 'four', also known as *walking bass* lines, is actually quite simple, as it is a series of quarter notes. Like 'two'-playing, however, the feel is critical. Keep in mind the importance of the second and fourth beats in swing – a small accent on those beats is appropriate. Also, when imitating an acoustic bass, legato is very important. Example 10-3 illustrates a ii-V-I-V/ii progression and how a walking bass line functions. Since the object is to arrive on each chord tone on the beat that it occurs, the descending version of the line is simple – it's just a major scale. The ascending version – since it's an ascending fourth – requires a chromatic tone, close to the goal of the approaching chord change. Remember these examples provide only a framework for this process, and a complete discussion and analysis of bass lines is beyond the scope of this book. Listening to how bass players, and pianists, construct bass lines is critical.

Example 10-3   *Walking Bass Line (Playing in 'Four') – ii-V-I-V/ii*

One chord per measure:

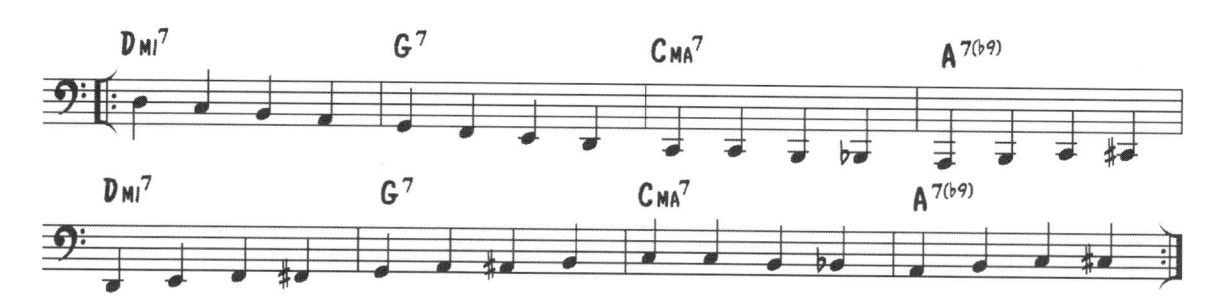

Two chords per measure:

Guided Learning Tune II illustrates a walking bass line. This would probably be used during the solos, so there is no melody notated in Example 10-4.

96   Part II: Rhythm and Style

Example 10-4 Guided Learning Tune II – Bass Line in 'Four'

Pedal Point

One of the ways in which bassists create tension and momentum is through the use of pedal points – where a tone is sustained through shifting harmonies. This often occurs during turnarounds with the dominant (V) bass note played in a variety of rhythms. Example 10-5 illustrates this technique, taking the content from Example 10-3 and establishing a pedal point at the end of the example.

Example 10-5 *Dominant Pedal Point – ii-V-I-V/ii*

Exercise 10-1: Bass Lines

Practice the ii-V-I-V/ii bass lines above, the bass lines in *Guided Learning Tune II*, and in standards.

Locked Hands

There is an important jazz piano style known as 'locked hands', which was popularized by Milt Buckner and especially by the better-known George Shearing. It is also a technique for arrangers. In its simplest form, it is constructed of a harmonized melody in four-way close voicings, with the left hand doubling the melody an octave below – thereby creating a five-voice structure. This is a common voicing for saxophone sections, where the baritone saxophone doubles the melody an octave below. This technique can also be used with drop-2 voicings, in which case the voicing structure is normally reduced to four voices (because the root would not be doubled).

This method can be used for any type of melody or improvised solo, but is especially useful in harmonizing stepwise lines that include passing tones (and other non-chord tones). Neighbor tones (those that move back and forth from the same chord tone) are often harmonized by *planing* – all voices moving in the direction of the melody. Passing tones (tones that move from one chord tone to another, creating step-wise motion) are often harmonized by simply using the current scale, or the 'key of the moment' by moving diatonically. Another approach for harmonizing passing tones is to use diminished chords. The use of diminished chords is useful in demonstrating, and perfecting, the locked hands style. Example 10-6 illustrates this method.

98   Part II: Rhythm and Style

Example 10-6 *Locked Hands, with Passing Diminished Seventh Chords, in Close and Drop-2 Voicings*

Notice that the top note of this passage is comprised of an eight-note scale – a C major scale with a flatted sixth. (Barry Harris has coined the term "sixth diminished scale" for this

Special Techniques 99

collection of notes). It is useful for this exercise, because the notes of the major six chord – C, E, G, and A – are all harmonized with a C6 chord. The other tones – D, F, A♭, and B – are all harmonized with the same diminished seventh chord. Also notice that the top system is in four-way close, the second in drop-two, the third in four-way close in minor, and the bottom system is in drop-two, also in minor.

Example 10-7 illustrates the locked hands method using *Guided Learning Tune I*. The example contains notes describing what is unfolding, but generally, you'll see that the melody is doubled in the left hand, unless the voicings are in drop-two; in those cases, there is a tenth between the outer voices.

Example 10-7 *GLT I with Locked Hands Voicings*

100 Part II: Rhythm and Style

> *Exercise 10-2:* **Locked Hands**
>
> Practice Example 10-6 in all keys. Then employ the technique in jazz standards – especially those with step-wise melodies, such as *Polka Dots and Moonbeams, There Will Never Be Another You, Fly Me To the Moon,* etc.

Red Garland Block Chord Method

The great pianist Red Garland employed a method similar to the locked hands style described above, but it differed in the follow ways: the right hand plays three notes – an octave plus one chord tone in the middle; and the left hand plays four-way close voicings or three note shell voicings. The hands play the same rhythms as in the locked hands style. Passing tones can be harmonized with diatonic or diminished harmony, or like in the example below, simply retain the same left hand voicing as the melody moves. Garland famously used this technique in the treatment of the melody in his great version of *Billy Boy*, but it is often used to supply energy in a solo. Soloists often use this method at the apex of a solo.

Example 10-8 Red Garland Block Chord Voicings Over the ii-V-I-V/ii Progression 🔊

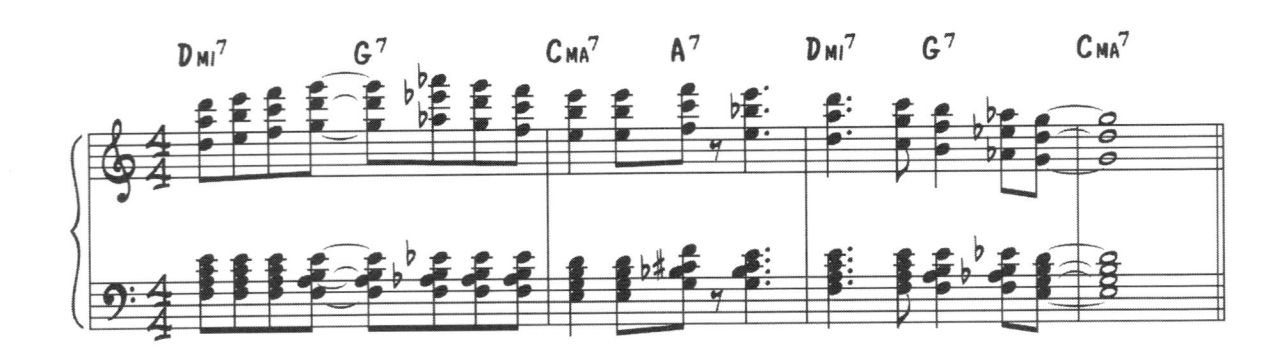

Example 10-9 illustrates the Red Garland block chord method using *Guided Learning Tune II*.

Special Techniques 101

Example 10-9 GLT II with Red Garland Block Chord Voicings

[Octave plus middle voice chord tone in RH]
[Four-way close LH Voicings]
[Three note shell voicing in LH here]

Exercise 10-3: Block Chords

Practice Example 10-8 in all keys. Then employ the technique in jazz standard melodies, such as *Autumn Leaves, Embraceable You, In a Mellow Tone,* etc.

102 Part II: Rhythm and Style

Stride

Stride refers to a style that was developed in U.S. east coast cities during the 1920s and 30s. It evolved from ragtime, where a solid left hand pattern of alternating bass notes and chords is placed under a syncopated right hand melody. There are important differences between ragtime and stride – stride is improvised music, while ragtime is notated, and stride is firmly rooted in the swing tradition, while ragtime's syncopations are sixteenth note figures (rather than a swing eighth note feel). Great stride players include James P. Johnson, Fats Waller, Willie "The Lion" Smith, Thelonious Monk, Duke Ellington, and Count Basie.

In situations where the harmonic rhythm is one measure per chord (in four-four time), stride is played by placing the root on beat one and the fifth on beat three, with chords appearing on beats two and four. Where the harmonic rhythm is two chords per four-four bar, the root is played on beat one, the chord on beat two, the root of the next chord on beat three, and the chord on beat four. Example 10-10 illustrates two stride patterns. The first one is a left-hand stride pattern with a harmonic rhythm of one chord per measure, the other where the harmonic rhythm is doubled. The first example illustrates another common technique – "walking tenths".

Example 10-10 Left-hand Stride Pattern

One Chord Per Measure:

[Walking tenths here]

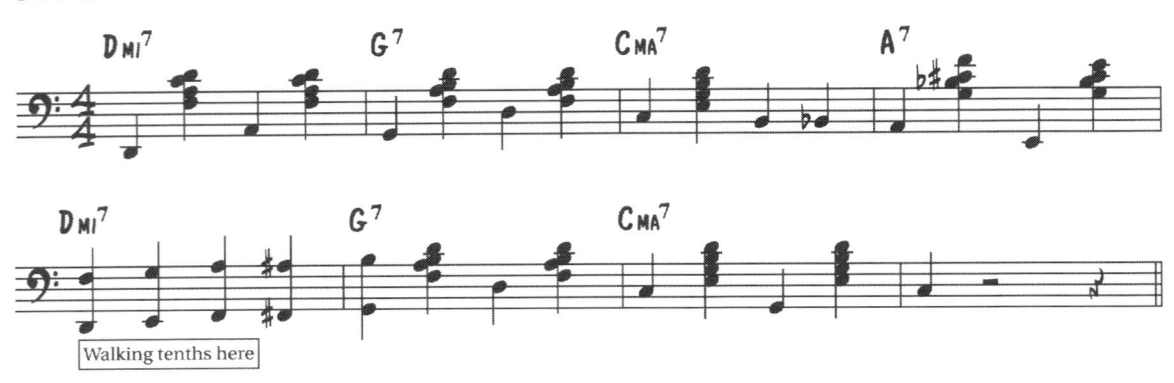

Two Chords Per Measure:

Example 10-11 illustrates *Guided Learning Tune I* with a stride accompaniment pattern.

Example 10-11 GLT I With Stride Left-Hand Accompaniment

Exercise 10-4: Stride

Practice Example 10-10, in both harmonic rhythms, in all keys. Add a right hand improvised line if possible. Then, employ the technique in jazz standard melodies, such as *Do You Know What It Means to Miss New Orleans, A Foggy Day*, the bridge section of *Don't Get Around Much anymore*, etc.

Boogie Woogie

Boogie woogie playing is a specialized field – just as there are blues musicians who don't consider themselves jazz musicians, there are pianists who largely limit their playing to boogie woogie. It is a useful tool to draw upon for all jazz pianists, however. This exciting style became popular during the 1920s and is largely associated with the blues. It is characterized by a repeating bass pattern that is hard-driving and assertive, and can be swung or played with a straight eighth-note feel. While there are many patterns associated with this style, Example 10-

104 Part II: Rhythm and Style

11 illustrates four of them:

Example 10-12 Boogie Woogie Bass Patterns Over an F chord

Example 10-13 illustrates *Guided Learning Tune II* in a boogie-woogie style. Like the version using modal planing (in Example 5-9), the chords have been simplified and a B♭7 chord has been added (to measure 10) to better match the style of old 'timey' or rock n' roll blues.

Example 10-13 GLT II in a Boogie Woogie Style.

Notice that different patterns have been used throughout. Normally, the same pattern would stay consistent throughout a tune. The purpose of the example is to illustrate several approaches.

> ### *Exercise 10-5:* Boogie Woogie
>
> Practice the left hand boogie woogie patterns in Example 10-12 in all keys.

This unit on rhythm and style is meant to convey the variety of possibilities open to jazz pianists – and also to amplify the need to be well-rounded in many approaches and styles. As a final piece of advice: try to play the same tune using the various approaches described above, including the diverse comping styles, locked hands, block chord, stride, and boogie woogie. You'll find that being flexible will make you a much better pianist.

Part III
The Improvised Line

The challenge and difficulty of jazz improvisation – of creating melodies spontaneously, within an often- complex harmonic system – is obvious to anyone who has attempted it. There is a misconception, especially among non-jazz musicians, that jazz musicians develop ideas organically that flow naturally with no preparation. This is of course not the case. As is true of voicings and chord progressions, scales and brief melodic lines can be practiced and memorized and then used to create tuneful and effective melodies, providing a foundation for creative thought. These short lines are often referred to as jazz *patterns*, or melodic *formulae*. A word of caution, however; we don't want to merely be 'pattern-machines', robotically playing practiced ideas that we know will 'fit'. It is best to work on patterns that develop a concept and assist in the creation of longer melodic spans.

Part III is divided into two chapters. Chapter 11 explores scales and melodic formulae that correspond to individual harmonies. Chapter 12 illustrates formulae that function over progressions. The reader should reference the scale summary found in Appendix A, as its understanding is important to grasp the concepts introduced here. This section offers only a sample of this vast topic, as there are additional scale choices and hundreds of patterns that can be employed. There are jazz improvisation method books that go much deeper than what is presented here, and the internet is full of helpful websites to help with the improvised line. This section will hopefully lead to more exploration.

11

Scales and Melodic Formulae for Individual Harmonies

The examples below present scales and several melodic formulae for use over major, minor, half diminished, and dominant sevenths utilizing diatonic, melodic minor, and diminished harmonic systems. While it is important to connect chords as harmony progresses, which will be presented in Chapter 12, it is also useful to understand the sounds that work for each individual chord.

Major Seventh Chords - Scales

The first three examples include the major scale, the lydian mode, and the lydian-augmented scale, which is the third melodic minor mode. The major scale should be used for tonic chords in major and the III in minor. The lydian should be used for the IV chord in major and VI in minor, but also works to brighten a tonic (I) chord. The lydian-augmented scale works well for tonic chords with a raised fifth.

Example 11-1 *Major, Lydian, and Lydian-Augmented Scales*

One of the primary advantages of using pentatonic scales is the *elimination* of notes from a seven-note scale. Note that in Example 11-2, the scale based upon the root includes the root, second (or ninth), third, fifth, and sixth, but does not include the seventh. This would be useful over a major 6 chord, where the seventh is to be avoided. The pentatonic built upon the fifth includes the fifth, sixth (or thirteenth), seventh, second (or ninth), and third of the Cma7, but excludes the root and fourth – two dissonant tones in a major seventh chord. The pentatonic built on the second scale degree includes the second (or ninth), third, ♯11, sixth (or thirteenth), and the seventh. It excludes the root and fifth.

Example 11-2 Pentatonic Scales: Based on the root, fifth, and second.

Major Seventh Chords - Melodic Formulae

Major sevenths are normally 'inside' chords; patterns that emphasize colorful chord tones, like sevenths, thirds, and ninths, work well. Double neighbor motion, or *enclosures* are extremely common in jazz lines. The following pattern surrounds the root of the chord with the ninth (D) and seventh (B). Note that the pattern begins on the fifth of the chord.

Example 11-3 Major Seventh Pattern

Formulae that fit comfortably under the hand can be of great use to pianists. The pattern shown in Example 11-4 is one such formulae. Note that there is no chord symbol indicated; this short gesture could be used for multiple harmonic situations – a Cadd9, an Ami11 Fma9, B♭ma13(♯11), A♭ma7(♯5), and Dmi11 are a few examples, and it is illustrated with all of these possibilities in the audio example. It is included in this 'major' section as its construction is based on a Cadd9 chord.

Example 11-4 Flexible Add-9 Pattern

Scales and Melodic Formulae: 113
Individual Harmonies

Minor Seventh Chords - Scales

Examples below include dorian, phrygian, aeolian, melodic minor, pentatonic, and blues scales.

The ii Chord in Major, iv Chord in Minor

Example 11-5 Dorian Mode

Example 11-6 Minor Pentatonic

The minor blues scale can be used over a major or minor blues progression, but it can also be used over a minor seventh chord. It is also a very common scale for use of a i-IV7 dorian progression – as in, Cmi7-F7.

Example 11-7 Minor Blues Scale

114 Part III: The Improvised Line

The iii Chord in Major

Example 11-8 *Phrygian Mode*

The vi Chord in Major

Example 11-9 *Aeolian Mode (Natural Minor)*

The i Chord in Minor

Example 11-10 *The Melodic Minor Scale*

Minor Seventh Chords - Melodic Formulae

Quartal motion, as with quartal voicings, provide a spacious, angular sound. The following pattern, which is derived from the dorian mode, begins on the root of the chord, leaps to the fourth, moves down in thirds to the chord fifth, then leaps again up a fourth. It also provides an example of a *triad pair* (two triads with no notes in common that form a pattern). There is a G minor triad beginning on beat two, followed by an F major triad beginning on the 'and of three'. It can also be used for suspended chords because it emphasizes the fourth and omits the third.

Example 11-11 *Minor Seventh and Sus 4 Pattern*

[Musical notation: Cmi7 and C7sus]

Playing outside the harmony creates tension and excitement. One way to approach this important concept is play an inside pattern with the right hand and move the left hand in and out of the harmony. Example 11-12 illustrates this with a minor pentatonic four-note pattern in the right hand and left hand quartal voicings that, in the first two measures, reflect the dorian mode but move chromatically, and therefore 'outside', in the third and fourth measures. Also, take note of the low open fifths in the left hand – a technique reminiscent of McCoy Tyner.

Example 11-12 *Inside/Outside Playing*

[Musical notation: Cmi7]

LH: Inside the Dorian Mode   LH: Outside, Chromatic Side-slipping

Half-Diminished Chords - Scales

Half-diminished chords function as ii chords in minor and vii in major. The scales for this chord include locrian and locrian ♮2 (the sixth mode of the ascending melodic minor system). Note that the locrian ♮2 includes the ninth in the chord symbol. A melodic formulae example for half-diminished chords will be presented in the next chapter, as part of a ii-V-I progression.

Example 11-13 Locrian and Locrian ♯2 Scales

Dominant Seventh Chords – Dual Roles

It is useful to think of dominant seventh chords as either *resolving* or *non-resolving*. Resolving dominants – those that participate in a V-I or V-i, or any falling fifth motion - can include chord tone substitutes (and melodic lines) that are either bright or dark. Darker, or more dissonant, chord tones and scale choices will result in a more urgent resolution. Dominants that don't resolve down by a fifth work well with bright chord tones.

Some scales, such as mixolydian and dominant bebop, work well for both instances. Others have more specific roles: half-whole diminished, mode V harmonic minor, and super locrian are excellent 'resolving' scales. Non-resolving dominants sevenths - for example, tritone substitutes, backdoor dominants, or simply non-functional dominants - should normally include chord tone substitutes (and melodic lines) that are bright (since they are not part of a resolution). The brightest dominant scale is the lydian-dominant, which is the fourth mode of melodic minor. Finally, the major blues scale has a specific role and purpose, as the blues has a unique harmonic language (i.e., the tonic chord is a normally dominant seventh chord).

Dominant Seventh Chords – Scales

Mixolydian, Dominant Bebop, Major Blues, Half-Whole Diminished, Mode V Harmonic Minor, Super Locrian, Lydian-Dominant

Mixolydian

The mixolydian mode, being the fifth mode of a major scale, is the most 'inside' choice for a dominant seventh. It can be used for both resolving and non-resolving dominants.

Example 11-14 Mixolydian Mode

SCALES AND MELODIC FORMULAE: 117
Individual Harmonies

Dominant Bebop

The dominant bebop scale – especially when it descends – is an extremely useful scale. The dominant bebop scale is constructed of eight notes, and includes both the major and minor seventh. As you practice Example 11-15, notice that the primary chord tones – root, seventh, fifth, and third - appear on the strong beats when the scale descends. It can also be used for both types of dominants.

Example 11-15 *Dominant Seventh Bebop Scale Pattern*

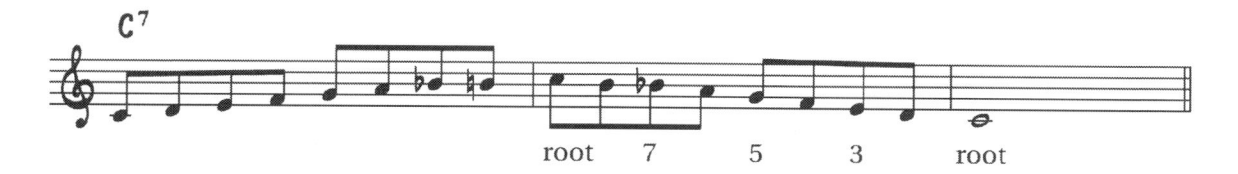

Exercise 11-16 illustrates an effective way to practice bebop scales. Note that since the scale is constructed of eight notes, an octave is reached on the downbeat of the subsequent measure. The exercise focuses upon building the scale beginning and ending on the root, third, fifth, and seventh.

Example 11-16 *Dominant Seventh Bebop Scale Pattern – Chord Tone Emphasis*

Major Blues

As mentioned above, the dominant seventh chord is used as a tonic chord in the blues – this is what makes the blues a unique harmonic environment. Both the minor and major blues scales can be used over the blues progression. Example 11-7 illustrates the minor blues scale, as it can also be used over minor chords. Example 11-17 contains the major blues scale. Note the presence of the minor and major thirds.

118 Part III: The Improvised Line

Example 11-17 Major Blues Scale

It was previously stated that the mixolydian and dominant bebop scales work well in both resolving and non-resolving situations. The scales presented below are more specifically designed to create tension and resolve.

Half-Whole Diminished

The diminished scale is a powerful tool in the hands of jazz improvisers. This scale of alternating half and whole steps offers opportunities to create angular and musical lines that work well over a resolving dominant seventh chord. It is important to realize that the fully diminished chord and the dominant seventh flat nine chord are identical. (For example, an E diminished seventh is constructed of an E, G, B♭, and D♭. A C dominant flat nine chord is constructed of the root, E, G, B♭, and D♭). The proper scale choice for a fully diminished chord is a whole-half diminished. (For example, using E as the root, the notes are: E-F♯-G-A-B♭-C-D♭-E♭). That same scale can be employed over a dominant flat nine chord, as is illustrated below. The scale's color in relation to a dominant seventh comes from the presence of the major 13th – the A, and the altered ninths – the D♭ and E♭ (enharmonic equivalent to D♯).

Example 11-18 Half-Whole Diminished Scale

Mode V Harmonic Minor

The V chord generated by the minor scale system involves chord tones that include the flat and sharp ninths and the flatted thirteenth, along with the root, third, and seventh. The harmonic minor scale is an excellent 'inside' choice for dominant chords functioning in a minor key as it clearly reflects the prevailing minor harmony. Note the distinctive augmented second between the D♭ and E.

Example 11-19 Mode V Harmonic Minor

Super Locrian

The super locrian mode (seventh mode of the ascending melodic minor scale system), is another excellent choice for the dominant chord in minor keys. Example 11-20 illustrates this mode; note the colorful altered ninths, the ♯11, and ♭13. It is also known as the "altered scale".

Example 11-20 Super Locrian, or "Altered"

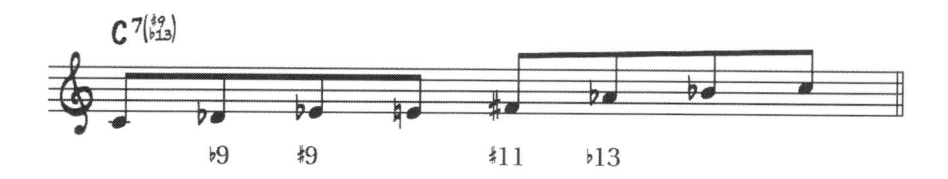

Lydian-Dominant

The lydian-dominant mode works especially well for non-resolving dominant sevenths. This bright scale includes the raised fourth and lowered seventh. Since it is a melodic minor mode, it shares the same notes as the super locrian mode a tritone away. So a C lydian-dominant is equivalent to a G♭ super locrian mode. The raised fourth (the F♯ in Example 11-21) has a tendency for upward motion to the fifth (the G). Note that the example includes a second measure where the scale descends; the fourth is lowered to an F, as it resolves to the third (the E).

Example 11-21 Lydian-Dominant

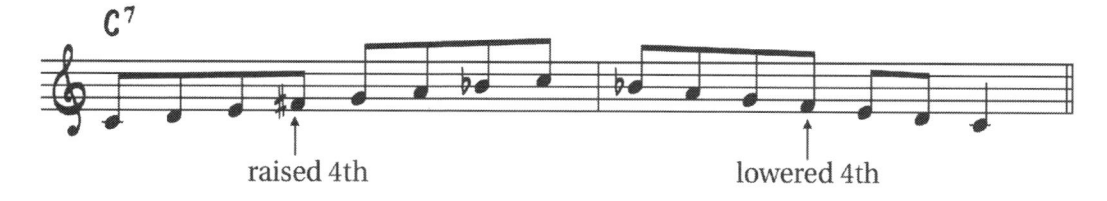

Resolving and Non-Resolving Dominant Melodic Formulae

Example 11-22 is constructed of the bebop scale (note the major seventh B natural and the minor seventh B flat), and also includes a sharp 4th (or 11th) – the F♯ in the second measure - which is an important element of the lydian-dominant scale. The F♯ is lowered in the second measure as the line progresses downward, as was seen in Example 11-21. It can be used as both a resolving and non-resolving dominant seventh.

Example 11-22 Non-Resolving Dominant Seventh Pattern – Bright

Example 11-23 illustrates a very common – one could say over-used – pattern that utilizes notes of the super locrian, or *altered* melodic minor mode in a V-i progression. This is a simple pattern to play on the piano, as it fits well under the fingers. The pattern is constructed of a minor triad built on the tone a half step up from the root of the chord – plus the second degree of that triad. Example 11-23 is constructed of a D♭ minor triad with an added E♭. These tones of course are enharmonically altered ninths and the A♭ is the flatted thirteenth.

Example 11-23 Resolving Dominant Seventh Pattern – Dark

Example 11-24 illustrates a pattern that works well with non-resolving dominants. It includes tones of the lydian-dominant scale, prominently features the thirteenth and raised eleventh, and begins with the enclosure figure.

Example 11-24 Lydian-Dominant Seventh Pattern

Scales and Melodic Formulae: 121
Individual Harmonies

Example 11-25 illustrates two common four note groups of the half-whole diminished scale. Notice that the chord generated by this scale is a 13th with a lowered ninth. As mentioned above, this kind of sequential pattern works well when resolving; however, it is often heard over non-resolving dominant sevenths as well.

Example 11-25 *Half-Whole Diminished Four Note Pattern*

The next example features a pattern extracted from a Joey Calderazzo solo. Note that it features many of the concepts discussed thus far: pentatonic usage, side-slipping, and quartal left hand voicings. This is a good example of a modal setting of a dominant seventh.

Example 11-26 *Major Pentatonic Side-Slipping Pattern Over Quartal Side-Slipping*

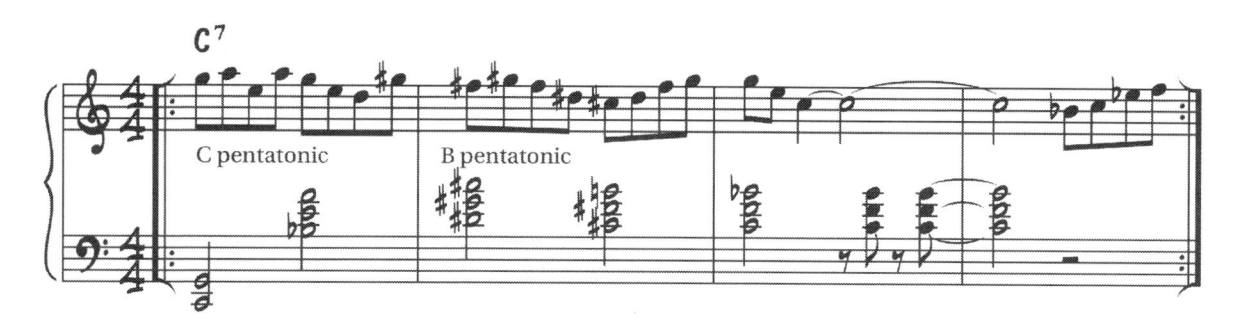

LH: Quartal Stacks

122 Part III: The Improvised Line

Improvising with Various Rhythmic Values: The Challenge of Sixteenth Notes

The examples presented in this chapter are mostly constructed of eighth note lines. Jazz improvisors of course use a variety of rhythmic values. Quarter notes (including the occasional quarter note triplet), eighth notes, eighth note triplets, and sixteenth notes are all used in combination. Obviously, faster note values tend to create excitement and drive, but are most effective in combination with slower note values.

Improvising with eighth note triplets in a tune that swings (rather than Latin) feels natural because the eighth note triplet resembles swing eighth notes. However, sixteenth notes present a challenge, because they don't technically 'swing', but are played 'straight'.

The last example of this chapter offers a practice method to gain fluency in improvising with changing rhythm values, and especially will help with sixteenth note lines. Example 11-27 contains a G dorian mode, where the scale is played first in eighths, then in eighth note triplets, then in sixteenths as the scale ascends. The descending scale works the same way.

Example 11-27 Scale Practice with Eighths, Eighth-Note Triplets, and Sixteenths

> ***Exercise 11-1*: Scales and Melodic Formulae for Single Harmonies**
>
> - Scales and Modes:
>   - Practice and memorize, hands together, four octaves, all keys, circle of fourths
>   - Practice and memorize, in the right hand alone, with the corresponding chord in the left hand, all keys, circle of fourths
> - Melodic Formulae
>   - Practice and memorize, hands together, four octaves, all keys, circle of fourths
>   - Practice and memorize, in the right hand alone, with the corresponding chord in the left hand, all keys, circle of fourths

12

Scales and Melodic Formulae over Common Progressions

Jazz improvisers are able to move between playing inside the harmony by either generalizing the harmony, as when playing a major scale over a ii-V-I progression without regard to the chord movement, or specifically adhering to the harmonic motion, where the chord sequence can be heard in the line. Further, experienced players know when it is appropriate to move outside (and back inside) the harmony. While this chapter focuses on harmonic specificity, the first example is constructed of the dorian, mixolydian, and major scales beginning on the roots of the ii, V, and I chords. This foundational exercise is useful in establishing the root movement and the appropriate 'inside' scale choices.

Example 12-1 *Dorian, Mixolydian, Major Scales over the ii-V-I Progression*

Jazz improvisation method books focus on the ii-V-I progression when demonstrating harmonic specificity, and this chapter will take that same approach. The progression comes in two primary types (in four/four time) – those with a harmonic rhythm of one chord per measure, and those that move twice as quickly, with the ii and V chords lasting two beats, and the I a full bar. In either case, the motion of the sevenths resolving to the thirds is the primary goal. This was also demonstrated with chord progressions, in Chapters 2, 4, and 6, and it is based on the same premise – but in a linear fashion. As in the voicing chapters, these will be referred to as *guide tones.* Finally, the patterns below will include bright and dark options, as seen with the single harmony patterns in Chapter 11.

Examples 12-2 through 12-5 are based upon the highly organized approach put forth by

Bert Ligon in his book about linear harmony[1]. In it, resolutions of sevenths as they move to thirds is codified into three 'outlines'. The examples resemble Ligon's, but are more rhythmically active than what he presents.

One Chord per Four/Four Measure Harmonic Rhythm

Example 12-2 is constructed of the guide tone seventh of the ii moving to the guide tone third of the V. The third of the V then becomes the seventh of the I. This illustrates the seventh-third resolution at its most basic level.

Example 12-2 Guide Tone Resolution

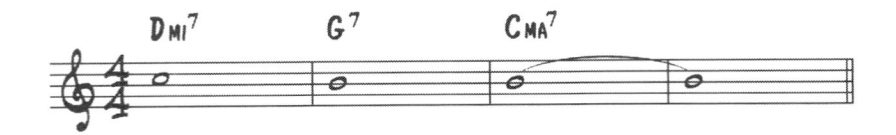

Example 12-3 expands on the previous example by using a descending scale – but keeping the seventh-third resolution. Ligon labels this 'Outline #1'. In this example, the seventh-third motion is duplicated when the V moves to I (the F of the G7 moving to the E of the Cma7).

Example 12-3 Guide Tone Resolution, with Scale

Example 12-4 is constructed of an arpeggio of the ii, followed by a guide tone resolution. This motion is identified by Ligon as 'Outline #2.'

Example 12-4 ii Chord Arpeggio, Guide Tone Resolution

---

[1] Ligon, Bert, *Connecting Chords with Linear Harmony* (Lebanon, IN: Houston Publishing, Inc. 1996), 6-9.

Scales and Melodic Formulae: 127
Common Progressions

Example 12-5 illustrates a common motion where the guide tone motion from ii-V is embellished by chromatic enclosure motion as the seventh of the ii moves to the third of the V. This resembles Ligon's 'Outline #3. This example also includes a turnaround chord of A7, so repeat signs are included, as the A7 will resolve back to the Dmi7. This progression was first seen in Example 4-5, (and this turnaround chord could be used with all of these patterns).

Example 12-5 *Guide Tone Resolution with a Chromatic Enclosure*

The next examples add more complexity and chromaticism. Example 12-6 uses tones of the half-whole diminished scale over the V chord.

Example 12-6 *Diminished Scale over the V Chord*

It is useful to practice melodic formulae that illustrate 'inside' playing vs. 'outside' playing. The following example contains two ii-V-I progressions; there is a bebop scale throughout measure two, over the first G7, which is 'inside' the major harmony; the bebop scale is converted to a super locrian mode for the second G7, halfway through the measure, which adds tension and momentum. Note that there is a flatted thirteenth (the E♭ on beat 3) and raised and lowered ninths (on beat four and on the 'and of four' - the B♭ and A♭). Notice also the chord symbols; the second occurrence of the G7 suggests a G altered chord to correspond to the chord tones generated by the super locrian mode.

128 Part III: The Improvised Line

Example 12-7 *Bebop and Bebop + Superlocrian over the V Chord*

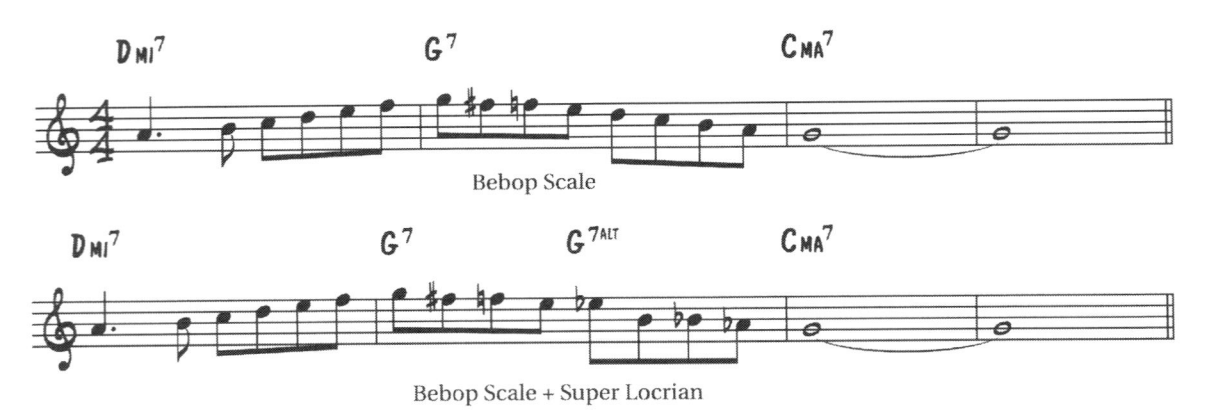

Bebop Scale

Bebop Scale + Super Locrian

More chromaticism and enclosures are utilized in the colorful pattern in Example 12-8. The first line is also seen in Example 11-22.

Example 12-8 *Colorful Enclosure-based Pattern*

A formulae introduced in Chapter 11 (Example 11-4, labeled as "Flexible Add-9 Pattern") can be sequenced as part of a side-slipping, highly chromatic pattern. Example 12-9 illustrates this idea in two ways: one, beginning on the fifth of the ii chord, and; two, beginning on the fourth of the ii. The ascending chromatic motion creates tension but also a great deal of momentum. The 'wrong' notes over the dominant (and the C♯ over the Cma7) work well because of the strength of the motion.

Example 12-9 *Sequenced "Add-9" Pattern*

Scales and Melodic Formulae: 129
Common Progressions

It is important to be as comfortable in minor keys as well as major. Minor progressions offer more options because of the variability of the available minor scales. The following examples illustrate formulae over the ii-V-i progression in minor. Examples 12-10 and 12-11 are identical to Examples 12-3 and 12-4, but are in minor.

Example 12-10 Guide Tone Resolution, with Minor Scale

Example 12-11 ii Chord Arpeggio, Guide Tone Resolution, in Minor

The next example uses tones of the melodic minor mode system. The locrian ♮2 mode is used for the ii chord and the super locrian mode is used for the V.

Example 12-12 Minor ii-V-i with Melodic Minor Modes

Example 12-13 is a very useful exercise, in that it demonstrates three melodic minor modes using the same shape in the form of a sequence – locrian ♮2 over the ii, super locrian over the V, and melodic minor over the i chord.

Example 12-13 Minor ii-V-i, with Sequenced Melodic Minor Modes

Borrowed Harmony and Secondary Function

Secondary dominants are used to increase motion, since a dominant chord is by its nature dissonant. Often, a ii chord is substituted by a V of V – essentially thinking of the ii chord as the dominant of the subsequent V chord. As we learned in constructing voicings, borrowing from minor is a common technique used in all kinds of music. In Example 12-14, these concepts are combined: the Dmi7 is transformed into a D7 (the V of G), and includes tones of the super locrian melodic minor mode – note the raised and lowered ninths which are part of that scale. Since the super locrian is used often as a scale choice for the dominant in a minor key, we hear the D7 as the dominant of G minor. Note that the raised and lowered ninths of the G7 chord are also used, creating a sequence.

Example 12-14 Borrowed Harmony/Secondary Function Pattern

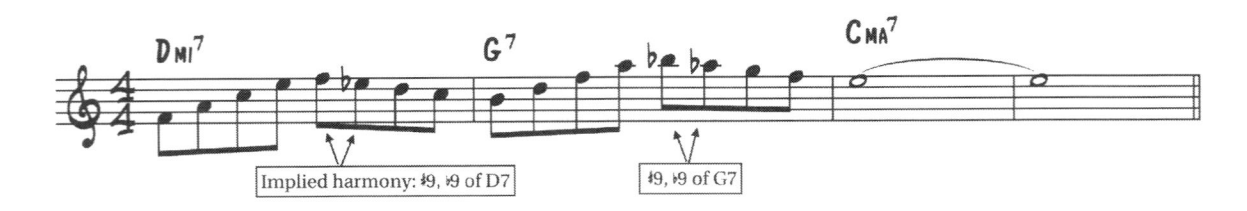

Two chords per Four/Four Measure Harmonic Rhythm

This next section is constructed of similar shapes and resolutions as the previous material, but the harmonic rhythm is doubled. Pianists need to be comfortable with creating lines that outline the harmony no matter the pace of the chord changes. Example 12-15 combines the shapes seen earlier in Examples 12-3 and 12-4, moving twice as fast.

Example 12-15 Guide Tone Resolutions, Faster Harmonic Rhythm

A fundamental goal when improvising a line is arriving on chord tones – also known as *target notes* – just as the chords appear rhythmically. The next example offers a useful tool to assist in

achieving this goal. By beginning on the root, third, fifth, or seventh of a ii chord, and playing an ascending eighth note scale, chord tones of the I chord will be reached just as that chord appears rhythmically.

Example 12-16 Target Note Exercise

The next pattern is a useful exercise as training for the ubiquitous I-vi-ii-V progression, found in many standards. It is also the foundation for *rhythm changes.*

Example 12-17 I-vi-ii-V Pattern

Improvising with Various Rhythmic Values Over a ii-V-I: The Challenge of Sixteenth notes.

The last example in the previous chapter – Example 11-27 – illustrates a method for gaining fluency with a variety of rhythmic values. It is mentioned there that sixteenth notes present a unique challenge, because they are played with a straight feel, rather than swung. They present a further challenge, however. The resolutions and target note practice that you have diligently drilled will work out differently when using sixteenths. Therefore, working on hitting target notes at the appropriate time takes additional practice when using sixteenth notes. Example 12-18 presents ii-V-I lines illustrating three rhythmic values: eighth notes, eighth note triplets, and sixteenth notes. Note that the shape of the line is similar in each case, and the diminished scale is used for the dominant chord (hence the use of the 13(♭9) chord).

Example 12-18 *Progression Practice with Eighths, Eighth-Note Triplets, and Sixteenths*

> ### Exercise 12-1: Scales and Melodic Formulae over Common Chord Progressions
>
> - Scales and Modes:
>   - Practice and memorize, hands together, four octaves, all keys, circle of fourths
>   - Practice and memorize, in the right hand alone, with the corresponding chord progression in the left hand, all keys, circle of fourths
> - Melodic Formulae
>   - Practice and memorize, hands together, four octaves, all keys, circle of fourths
>   - Practice and memorize, in the right hand alone, with the corresponding chord progression in the left hand, all keys, circle of fourths

Part IV
Creating a Performance

Throughout this book, *Guided Learning Tunes* are used to illustrate voicings, comping patterns, and piano-specific techniques. This last unit provides information about how to begin and end a tune, how to create transitional material, and it concludes with fully notated versions of the *Guided Learning Tunes.* These merely provide one way to approach these tunes; the possibilities are endless. You'll notice that material already introduced – some of the voicings, for example – are used again here.

13

Creating Transitional Material

Rhythm section members improvise throughout a performance, as voicings, chord tone substitutions, and comping rhythms are created. Horn players also improvise beyond their featured solo, because melodies are interpreted individually. In fact, fake book melodies are often written in such a basic manner – a long series of quarter notes for example, to make them easy to sight-read – that interpretation is a must. Since jazz standards are usually divided into distinct sections – the common song forms of AABA and ABAC are highly sectional - jazz musicians must be able to connect these sections, thereby creating a cohesive performance. Also, the melodies of blues tunes are normally played twice – so again, a transition must be created between the two melodic statements. This chapter offers examples of transitional material using the *Guided Learning Tunes*.

Adding transitional material normally involves creating momentum over 'turnaround' progressions – those series of chords that either return to something already heard, or move on to new material (to a bridge section for example).

Chordal and Linear Methods

It is useful to conceive of transitional material in two ways: chordal, where the turnaround is voiced with a variety of chords and chord rhythms, and; linear, where a melodic line is improvised over the prevailing harmony. Obviously, the linear approach is available for all jazz instrumentalists and vocalists. The chordal approach can be employed by only pianists, guitarists, and arrangers.

Guided Listening Tune I will be used to illustrate the chordal method. Since *GLT I* is only constructed of an eight measure progression, the example will illustrate a return to the beginning of the form.

138 Part IV: Creating a Performance

Example 13-1 *GLT I with Chordal Transition Material*

[Musical notation: Med. Swing, with chords Cma7, B♭mi7, E♭7, A♭ma7, Dø, G7(♭9), Cmi7, Dø, G7, Cma7, A7(♭9), F#/A, Dmi11, G7]

Transition consists of a slash chord - F#/A - and a *So What* voicing - Dmi11

    There are many other ways to achieve the goal of creating connective tissue using chordal transitional material. Be aware, however, that the top of whatever chords are used in the turnaround, will form a melody. In Example 13-1, the melody created (in the boxed area) begins with the E on top of the Cma7 chord, moving to the G eighth note, to the A♮, etc. Notice also that it has plenty of rhythmic momentum.

    Example 13-2 uses a linear material – a line that would be improvised – to return to the top of the form. *Guided Listening Tune II* is used for this illustration, and notice the use of chromaticism, upper extension arpeggio, and as seen in Example 13-1, rhythmic drive.

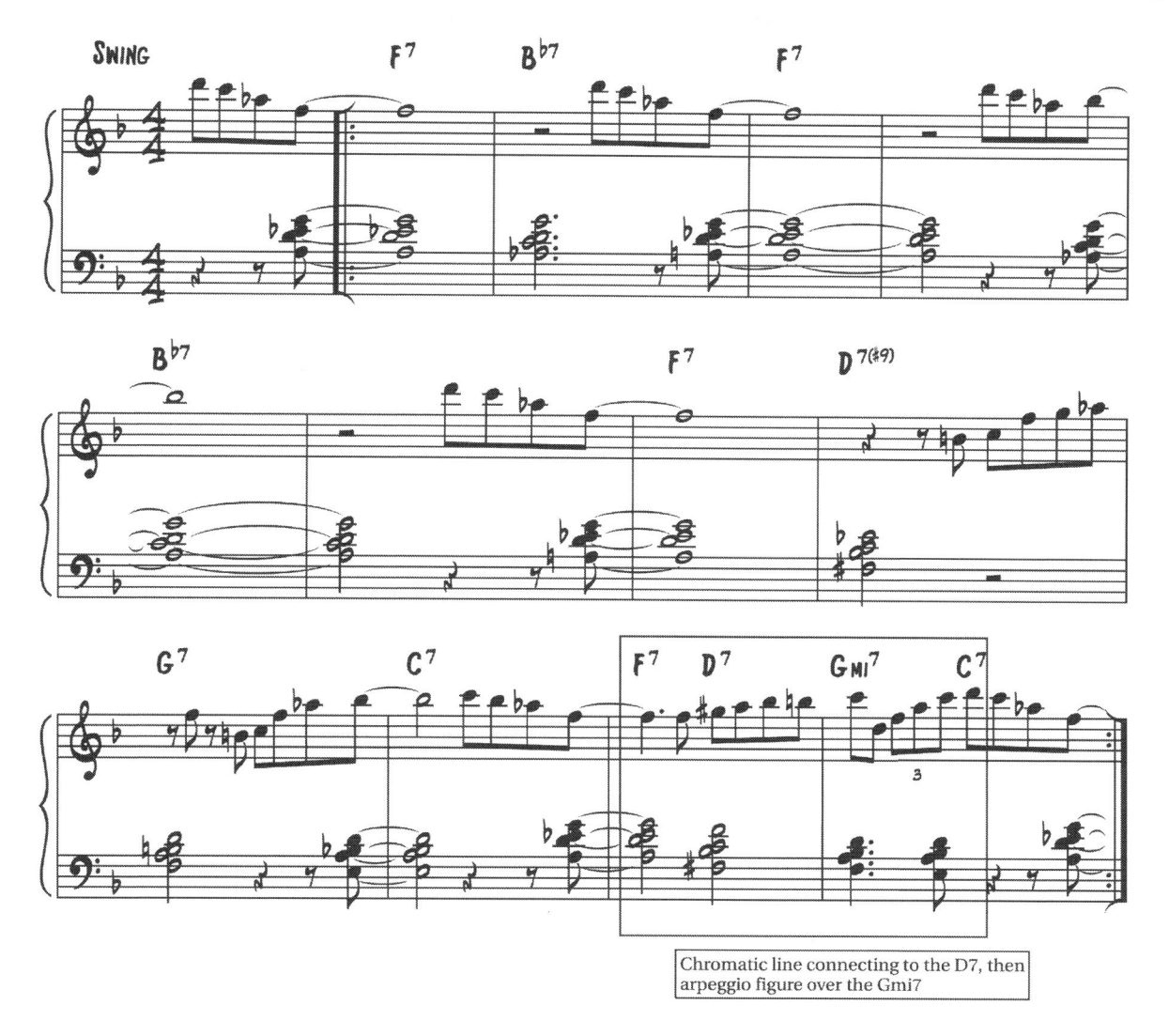

Creating Transitional Material 139

Example 13-2 *GLT II with Linear Transitional Material*

Chromatic line connecting to the D7, then arpeggio figure over the Gmi7

Again, there are endless options in creating lines to connect sections. A strong soloist – one who can create tuneful and logical lines while improvising – will also be a successful performer of jazz melodies and will be able to create transitions. Practicing voicings and melodic formulae and using them musically in transitional sections is the best method for success. Finally, listening to great recordings with a focus on the transitions between sections is essential.

Exercise 13-1: Creating Transitions

Use either chords or lines to create transitional material in jazz standards.

14

Introductions

The introduction is vital to a performance as it is obviously the first musical event that occurs. The introduction needs to match the style, tempo, rhythmic feel, and overall essence of the tune to which it is attached. Not only does the introduction begin the piece, it is also likely that the material you choose for the intro will come back somewhere else in the arrangement you're creating, and also may serve as the material for the ending.

Common Introduction Types

- Last section of the melody (often the last four measures)
- Vamp (a repeating series of a few chords)
- Rubato, re-harmonized version of the melody
- Using an improvised solo as an introduction

Last Section of the Melody

GLT I is used to demonstrate the use of the last four measures of the melody leading to the top of the form. This method can be used as a solo pianist or within a group setting. It works particularly well when performing with other players, as the band is led into the beginning of the melody with clarity, and no one is required to 'count-in' the band. Example 14-1 assumes that the pianist is playing with a bassist.

142 Part IV: Creating a Performance

Example 14-1 GLT I, with Last Four Bars as Intro

The pianist may want to play the first melodic figures and chords in a rubato style, and then perform the last two bars – the Cma7-A7-Dmi7-G7 section – in solid time. Whether the entire four bars are played in time or just the last two, the bassist will clearly know when to enter.

Vamp

A vamp is a repeating series of just a few chords – often as little as two. There are countless possibilities but a few that are fairly standardized. There have been some examples already presented in the book - in Chapter 3 there is a Gma7-Fma7 vamp - the "jam session" progression. In Chapter 9 there are several examples of comping using vamps, over bossa novas, and in the montuno style. They are extremely common in Latin styles. Refer these examples to explore the process of vamping.

Introductions 143

To use a vamp, the pianist simply selects a simple progression – a repeating i-IV dorian progression for example-and sets up the rhythm and feel of the tune with it. The other members of the band can join in the vamp, or can enter when the form of the tune begins.

Example 14-2 illustrates a vamp using F7 and Bb7 in *GLT II*, creating a four-measure intro that works well for a blues progression.

Example 14-2 *GLT II, With a Vamp as Introduction*

Rubato, Re-harmonized Introduction

A very common method for introducing a tune is for the pianist to construct a rubato, richly harmonized solo arrangement. Normally, the end of this solo arrangement is played in time, thereby notifying the other players that the beginning of the melody is approaching. There are hundreds of excellent examples of this technique; Bill Evans' *Someday My Prince Will Come*, from *Portrait in Jazz* and Keith Jarrett's incredible treatment of *Autumn Leaves*, from *Live at the Blue Note* are two excellent examples. Example 14-3 re-visits the re-harmonization from Example 8-2. The chord symbols reflect the re-harmonization.

Example 14-3 *GLT I, with Non-Functional Re-Harmonization as Intro*

Using a Solo as an Introduction

Because the improvised jazz solo is such a fundamental part of jazz, it is sometimes appropriate to begin a performance with just 'blowing' over the chord changes. The effect is one of vitality and energy which captures the audience's attention immediately. There will not be an example presented here to illustrate this approach; it is simply the form repeated until the melody arrives.

Exercise 14-1: Introductions

Add the four introduction types discussed in Chapter 14 to standards such as *Autumn Leaves, As Time Goes By, Don't Get Around Much Anymore, Afternoon in Paris*, etc.

15

Endings

Of all the elements of a successful jazz performance, continuity is perhaps the most vital. A performance should unfold logically, from the introduction, through the head, the solos, back to the head and then to the ending. The ending is critical – it is the last element heard by the listener. Some tunes don't require an ending; they can simply end at the conclusion of the melodic form. Sometimes it makes sense to use the introduction as the ending – thus creating the aforementioned continuity. This chapter will include some stock endings that every jazz musician needs to know, and will explore a few methods to successfully conclude a performance.

Common Ending Types

- Stock endings
- Tag - Last section of the melody (often the last four measures), repeated three (or more) times
- Vamp (often borrowed from the introduction)

Stock Endings

A stock ending is a well-known ending that has, over a period of time, become a common means by which to end a tune. These antiquated but effective endings are often performed on club date jobs. The two most common stock endings are:

(a) The original ending of the Billy Strayhorn standard, *Take the A Train*
(b) The so-called "Basie ending", named for the pianist and bandleader William "Count" Basie.

These two endings are provided in the Example 15-1.

148 Part IV: Creating a Performance

Example 15-1 Stock Endings

The "A Train" ending is often played by the entire band. The "Basie" ending is usually played by only the pianist. Note the use of the three note drop-2 voicings.

Tag

The material that is repeated for a tag ending can vary according to the harmonic rhythm. In tunes like *Take the A Train* and *All of Me*, the harmonic rhythm at the end of the form is one chord per four/four measure and is often a ii-V-I.

Example 15-2 Harmonic Rhythm – One Chord Per Measure

Example 15-3 illustrates how tunes with a harmonic rhythm of one chord per measure could be 'tagged'. Note the use of the V/ii to turn the progression around each time and the "A Train" stock ending.

Endings 149

Example 15-3 Tagging with One Chord Per Measure

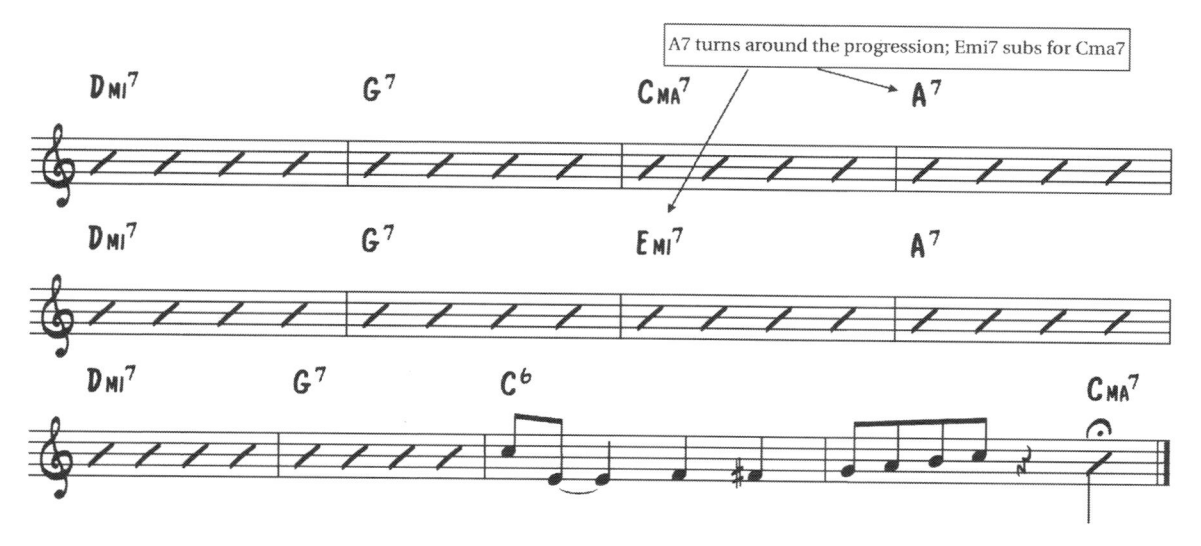

A similar process occurs when the harmonic rhythm is twice as fast. For example, in a progression such as I-vi-ii-V – popularized by the standard *I Got Rhythm,* the harmonic rhythm is two chords per measure.

Example 15-4 Harmonic Rhythm – Two Chords Per Measure

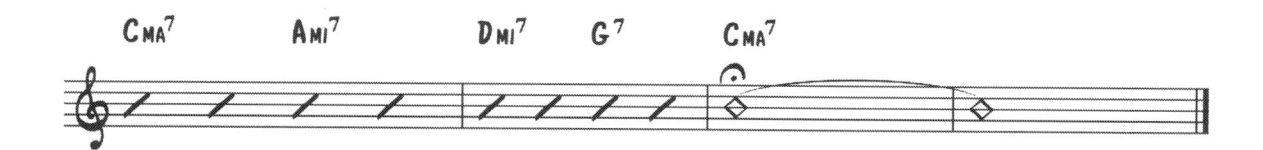

The third and fourth measures from the end are used for the tag in this case with the more rapid harmonic rhythm, and is illustrated below. The example concludes with the "Basie" stock ending.

Example 15-5 Tagging with Two Chords per Measure

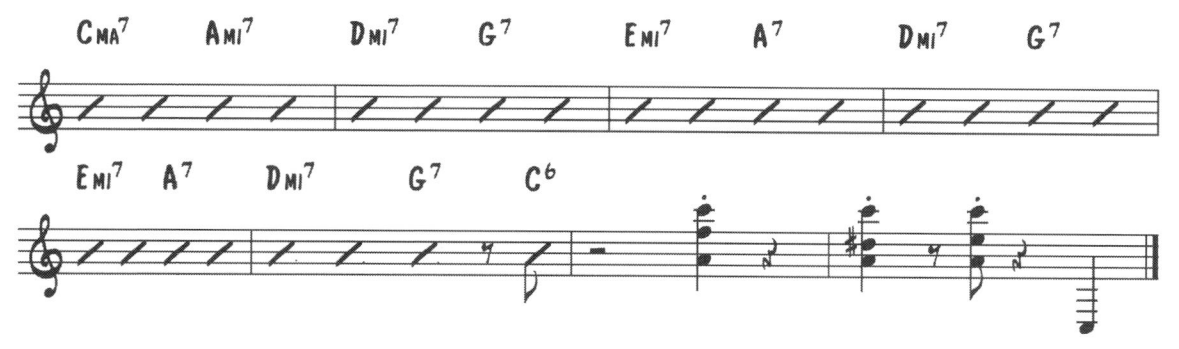

150 Part IV: Creating a Performance

Guided Learning Tune I will be used to illustrate a tag and stock ending. Example 15-6 below is based upon Example 4-9, where the melody is played by the right hand and chords are played by the left hand.

Example 15-6 *GLT I – Tagged Ending*

Vamp

Vamps are defined in the previous chapter as a repeated series of just a few chords. If a vamp is used as an introduction, that same vamp is often used for the ending. As mentioned earlier, this is a very common approach to Latin music. *GLT II* is used below to illustrate this method. The same vamp that was used as an introduction in Example 14-2 will be used for the ending.

152 Part IV: Creating a Performance

Example 15-7 *GLT II – Vamp Ending*

Note that the vamp begins in the tenth measure of the form; the turnaround has been eliminated. It is not needed, as the melody is not returning, and secondly, it is an interesting musical and formal effect to eliminate the turnaround and shorten the form.

> ### *Exercise 15-1:* Endings
>
> Add the three types of endings discussed in this chapter to standards, such as *Have You Met Miss Jones, A Foggy Day, Triste, etc.*

16

Guided Learning Tunes – Complete Versions

This final chapter presents the two *Guided Learning Tunes* as complete performances. They have introductions taken from those discussed in Chapter 14 and treatment of the melody from Chapters 4, 5, and 7. Comping techniques from Chapter 9 are used, as well as transitional material from Chapter 13, re-harmonization as seen in Chapter 8, and solos featuring melodic formulae described in Chapters 11 and 12. There are also some piano-specific effects illustrated in Chapter 10. Finally, the tunes have endings that were seen in Chapter 15. Much of what is shown here has been seen before; the concepts are now combined. Note that *GLT I* includes a bridge (only the A section was notated previously), and has a form of AABA. Only the piano parts are shown, though these versions are conceived of as trio performances – piano, bass, and drums.

Guided Learning Tune 1

Robert Larson

Swing ♩=120

A
CMA7
B♭MI7
E♭7
A♭MA7
D⌀
G7(♭9)
Left hand four-way close voicings
11
Bass and drums enter
CMI7
D⌀
G7
CMA7
AMI7
DMI7
G7
3
Transitional line connecting 'A' and 'B' sections
15
Locked hands in drop-two
B
CMA7
B♭MI7
E♭7
A♭MA7
19
Four-way close, left hand doubles the melody
D⌀
G7(♭9)
CMI7
D⌀
G7
CMA7
Drop-two on the G7, with a passing diminished chord on beat four.
22
Diminished chord on beat two.

C
Gmi7
C7
Fma7
Bb7sus
25
Cma7
F#mi7
B7
29
Ema7
G7sus
D
Cma7
Bbmi7
Eb7
33
Abma7
Dø
G7(b9)
Cmi7
Dø
G7
37

E
CMA7 AMI7 DMI7 G7 CMA7 BbMI7 Eb7
Solo
41
AbMA7 DØ G7 CMI7 DØ G7
3
7-3 resolution
45
DMI7 G7 CMA7
CMA7 A7
F
BbMI7 Eb7
49
AbMA7
DØ G7 CMI7
C minor blues pattern
53

160 Part IV: Creating a Performance

CMI7
D∅
G7
CMA7
A7
DMI7
G7
71
I
CMA7
B♭MI7
E♭7
A♭MA7
D∅
G7(♭9)
75
CMI7
D∅
G7
CMA7
AMI7
DMI7
G7
End of melody
79
CMA7
A7(♭9 ♭13)
DMI7
G7
EMI7
A7(♭9 ♭13)
DMI7
G7
C6
First tag
Second tag
83

162 Part IV: Creating a Performance

Guided Learning Tune II

Robert Larson

164 Part IV: Creating a Performance

D♭13(♯11)
C7sus
Minor pentatonic
33
C
F7
B♭7
F7
Piano solo
36
B♭7
F7
D7(♯9)
3
40
Gmi7
C7
F7
D7(♭9)
Gmi7
C7
3
44

F7
B♭7
F7
Bebop scale
3
48
B♭7
F7
D7(♯9)
52
Gmi7
C7
Superlocrian mode ('altered scale')
F7
D7(♭9)
Gmi7
C7
56
D
F7
B♭7
F7
Bass solo; piano voicings are open position
60

Bb7
F7
D7(#9)
64
Gmi7
C7
F7
D7(b9)
Gmi7
C7
"Red Garland" block chord 'shout' section
68
E
F7
Bb7
F7
72
Bb7
F7
D7(#9)
Three note shell voicing in LH here
76

168 Part IV: Creating a Performance

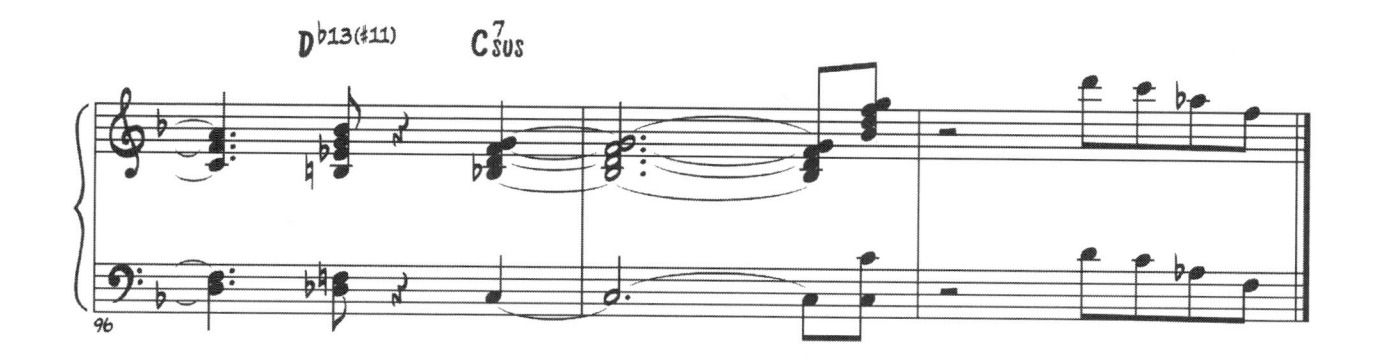

Appendices

A

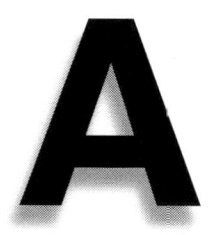

Chord/Scale Summary

The following chord/scale summary is divided into I chord scales, ii chord scales, and V chord scales, corresponding with the ii-V-I progression. Both the major and minor systems are included. There are also scales suggested for mediant, sub-mediant chords, an important non-resolving dominant scale, pentatonics, diminished, bebop and blues scales.

Chord/scales for Tonic Chords (I and i)

CMA7 — Ionian (major)

CMA7(♯5) — Lydian/augmented

CMI(MA7) CMI6/9 — Ascending melodic minor (Jazz minor)

Chord/scales for Supertonic Chords (ii and ii∅)

CMI7 — Dorian

C∅ — Locrian

C∅9 — Locrian ♮2

Chord/scales for Resolving Dominant Chords (V)

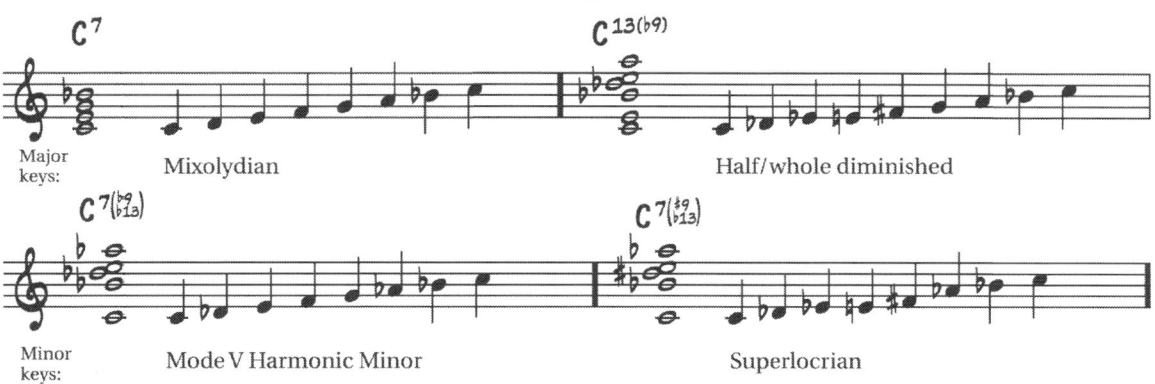

Major keys:

C7 — Mixolydian

C13(♭9) — Half/whole diminished

Minor keys:

C7(♭9/♭13) — Mode V Harmonic Minor

C7(♯9/♭13) — Superlocrian

Chord/scales for Non-resolving Dominant Chords

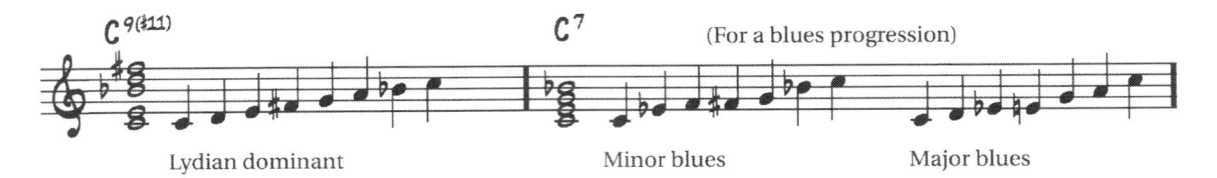

Lydian dominant

Minor blues (For a blues progression)

Major blues

Remaining Diatonic Modes - iii, IV, vi

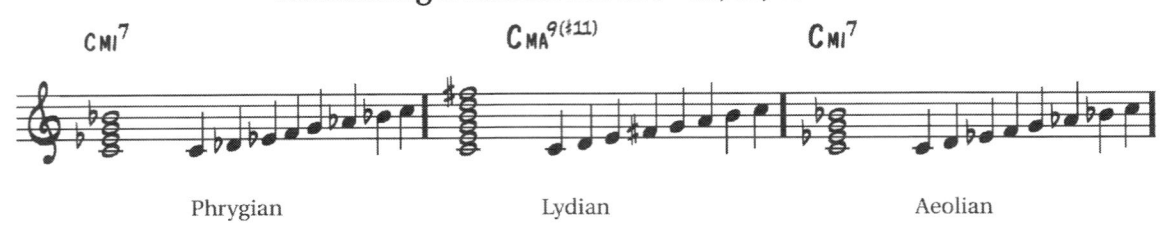

Phrygian

Lydian

Aeolian

Other Important Scales

Pentatonic

Whole/half diminished

Major Bebop

Minor Bebop

Dominant Bebop

B

Scale Fingerings

Scales are the foundation of technique, and proper fingering is critical for pianists regardless of genre or style. Solid fingerings are especially important for improvising musicians because as we improvise voicings and melodies, we improvise our fingering at the same time.

This section includes suggested fingerings for the following common-usage scales: Major, harmonic minor, ascending melodic minor, half-whole diminished, minor pentonic, and dominant bebop. The reason why the diatonic modes, melodic minor modes, whole-half diminished, and minor pentatonic are not included here is that those scales are derived from the scale fingers that you'll see below.

Finally, these are presented in a table format. Seeing them this way helps to categorize them in your mind. Of course, there are resources in classical and jazz piano books, technique methods, and of course, online.

Major
Hint: It is important to keep track of the location of the fourth finger, as it is used only once per octave

Right Hand Major scale	Fingering	Fourth Finger On:
C, D, E, G, A, B	1 2 3 1 2 3 4 5 (1…..)	7th
F	1 2 3 4 1 2 3 4 (1…..)	B♭
B♭	4 1 2 3 1 2 3 4	B♭
E♭	3 1 2 3 4 1 2 3	B♭
A♭	3 4 1 2 3 1 2 3	B♭
D♭	2 3 1 2 3 4 1 2	B♭
G♭	2 3 4 1 2 3 1 2	B♭
Left Hand Major Scale	**Fingering**	**Fourth Finger On:**
C, D, E, F, G, A	5 4 3 2 1 3 2 1	2nd
B♭, E♭, A♭, D♭	3 2 1 4 3 2 1 3	4th
G♭	4 3 2 1 3 2 1 2 (4…..)	Root
B	1 3 2 1 4 3 2 1	F♯

Harmonic and Melodic Minor

Right Hand Harmonic and Ascending Melodic Minor	Fingering	Fourth Finger On:
C, D, E, G, A, B	1 2 3 1 2 3 4 5 (1.....)	7th
F	1 2 3 4 1 2 3 4 (1.....)	B♭
B♭	4 1 2 3 1 2 3 4	B♭
E♭	3 1 2 3 4 1 2 3	B♭
A♭, D♭, G♭ (harmonic)	3 4 1 2 3 1 2 3	2nd
D♭, G♭ (melodic)	2 3 1 2 3 4 1 2	6th
Left Hand Harmonic and Ascending Melodic Minor		
C, D, E, F, G, A	5 4 3 2 1 3 2 1	2nd
B♭ (harmonic)	2 1 3 2 1 4 3 2	G♭
B♭ (melodic)	2 1 4 3 2 1 3 2	D♭
E♭	2 1 4 3 2 1 3 2	G♭
A♭, D♭	3 2 1 4 3 2 1 3	D♭
G♭	4 3 2 1 3 2 1 2 (4.....)	Root
B	1 3 2 1 4 3 2 1	F♯

Minor Pentatonic

Hint: using a pattern of groups of three and two works well. These fingers will also work with the relative major pentatonic scales.

Right Hand Minor Pentatonic	Fingering
C, G	1 2 1 2 3 1
D, E, F, A, B♭, E♭	1 2 3 1 2 1
B, A♭, D♭, G♭	2 1 2 3 1 2
Left Hand Minor Pentatonic	**Fingering**
C, D, E, F, G, A,	5 3 2 1 2 1
B	4 2 1 2 1 4
B♭, E♭	4 3 2 1 2 4
A♭	1 3 2 1 3 1
D♭	2 1 3 2 1 2
G♭	3 2 1 2 1

Half Whole Diminished

Hint: These scales can be grouped in a "C" group, an "F" group, and a "G" group. They played with the thumbs of both hands landing on the root, third, and fifth of each of those triad.

Right Hand Half-Whole Diminished	Fingering
C, E♭, G♭, A	C: 1 2 3 1 2 1 2 3 1
	E♭: 3 1 2 1 2 3 1 2 3
	G♭: 2 1 2 3 1 2 3 1 2
	A: 2 3 1 2 3 1 2 3
F, A♭, B, D	F: 1 2 3 1 2 1 2 3 1
	A♭: 3 1 2 1 2 3 1 2 3
	B: 2 1 2 3 1 2 3 1 2
	D: 2 3 1 2 3 1 2 1 2 3
G, B♭, D♭, E	G: 1 2 3 1 2 1 2 3 1
	B♭: 3 1 2 1 2 3 12 3
	D♭: 2 1 2 3 1 2 3 1 2
	E: 2 3 1 2 3 1 2 1 2
Left Hand Half-Whole Diminished	**Fingering**
C, E♭, G♭, A	C: 1 2 3 1 2 1 3 2 1
	E♭: 3 1 2 1 3 2 1 2 3
	G♭: 2 1 3 2 1 2 3 1 2
	A: 3 2 1 2 3 1 2 1 3
F, A♭, B, D	F: 1 3 2 1 2 1 3 2 1
	A♭: 2 1 2 1 3 2 1 3 2
	B: 2 1 3 2 1 3 2 1 2
	D: 3 2 1 3 2 1 2 1
G, B♭, D♭, E	G: 1 3 2 1 2 1 3 2 1
	B♭: 2 1 2 1 3 2 1 3 2
	D♭: 2 1 3 2 1 3 2 1 2
	E: 3 2 1 2 1 3 2 1 3

Dominant Bebop

Hint: For many of the scales, four-note groups works well.

Right Hand Descending Bebop	Fingering
C, D, E, F, G, A	5 4 3 2 1 4 3 2 1
B	3 2 1 3 2 1 3 2 1
B♭	2 1 3 2 1 3 2 1 2
E♭	4 3 2 1 4 3 2 1 4
A♭	2 1 2 1 3 2 1 3 2
D♭	3 2 1 4 3 2 1 4 3
G♭	2 1 4 3 2 1 4 3 2
Left Hand Descending Bebop	Fingering
C, D, E, F, G, A	1 2 3 4 1 2 3 4 1
B	1 2 1 2 3 1 2 3 1
B♭, E♭, A♭	3 1 2 1 2 3 1 2 3
D♭	3 4 1 2 3 4 3 2 1
G♭	4 1 2 3 4 1 2 3 4

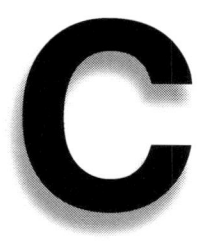

Jazz Theory Books

There are dozens of jazz theory books on the market, as well as hundreds of websites devoted to jazz theory and instruction. There are also resources devoted to improvisation, arranging, and hundreds of books designed for specific instruments. Piano and guitar method books are particularly useful as a primer for jazz theory concepts, and arranging texts are helpful with voicing concepts. Below is a brief annotated list of some excellent jazz theory and arranging books.

Bollin, Mark. *The Jazz Theory Workbook.* Rottenburg, Germany: Advance Music, 1993.

> This book contains information about theory basics, chord structures, chord/scale relationships, and chromaticism. It includes helpful exercises.

Degregg, Phil. *Jazz Keyboard Harmony: A Practical Method for All Musicians.* New Albany, IN: Jamey Aebersold Jazz, Inc., 1994.

> This text focuses mostly on chord voicings and exercises, containing graphical representations of voice-leading movement and dozens of exercises.

Dobbins, Bill. *Jazz Arranging and Composing: A Linear Approach.* Rottenburg, Germany: Advance Music, 1986.

> While the author methodically goes through writing for ensembles of various sizes, the strength of the book is the linear approach where melodies are harmonized in increasingly complex and interesting ways.

Fraedrich, Craig. Practical Jazz Theory for Improvisation. National Jazz Workshop Publications, 2014.

> This text, and its accompanying workbook, is meant to provide a foundation for jazz improvisers. It is designed for the beginner through advanced student and includes a suggested curriculum for jazz educators. It is organized for the self-learner as well as the classroom teacher.

Hyman, Dick. *Century of Jazz Piano.* Milwaukee, WI: Hal Leonard, 2012.

> This collection of important piano styles includes dozens of transcriptions with audio examples, focusing on major jazz piano innovations, including stride, boogie woogie, block chord playing, and modern techniques.

Jaffe, Andy. *Jazz Harmony.* Rottenburg, Germany: Advance Music, 1996.

This book includes important information about blues form, an intuitive analysis method, a strong chapter on modal borrowing, and the Coltrane matrix.

Levine, Mark. *The Jazz Piano Book.* Petaluma, CA: Sher Music, 1989.

This book contains theory material that is explained through the use of short transcribed passages, providing context for the content. It is comprehensive, in that voicings, chord/scale theory, comping are extensively covered.

Levine, Mark. *The Jazz Theory Book.* Petaluma, CA: Sher Music, 1995.

This comprehensive book includes hundreds of musical examples extracted from important jazz soloists, as well as a suggested repertoire list and listening suggestions. It is a fine companion book to Levine's piano book.

Ligon, Bert. *Jazz Theory Resources, Vol. 1 and 2.* Houston, TX: Houston Publishing, 200.

This two volume set includes analyses of several of the solos from Miles Davis' *Kind of Blue*, as well as excellent discussions of pentatonic usage, quartal harmony, and substitute harmony.

Lindsay, Gary. *Jazz Arranging Techniques, From Quartet to Big Band.* Miami, FL: Staff Art Publishing, 2005.

This comprehensive arranging book contains information about instrumentation, with recordings highlighting the tonal colors of various instrumental combinations and useful information about chord tone substitution.

Terefenko, Dariusz. *Jazz Theory: From Basic to Advanced Study*, 2nd edition. New York: Routledge, 2018

Terefenko, a professor at Eastman School of Music, has compiled a book for the beginner and advanced student. It includes an important chapter on phrase models and a chapter devoted to the innovative jazz pianist Lennie Tristano.

Tomaro, Mike & John Wilson. *Instrumental Jazz Arranging: A Comprehensive and Practical Guide.* Milwaukee, WI: Hal Leonard, 2009.

This is indeed comprehensive, with theory concepts, musical examples, audio examples, covering every conceivable instrumental combination. It can be used as personal text or in a classroom setting.

Wright, Rayburn. *Inside the Score.* Delevan, New York: Kendor, 1982.

> This remains the most informative and organized big band jazz arranging book on the market. This important book contains detailed analyses of arrangements by Sammy Nestico, Thad Jones, and Bob Brookmeyer, where voicings are extracted and carefully examined, explained, and categorized.

Select Discography

Compiling a discography of the history of jazz piano is another entire project (beyond this instruction book). Fortunately, there are jazz history books and online resources where recordings of great jazz pianists are listed, described, and evaluated. The purpose here is to simply identify some of my favorite recordings. This list obviously just barely scratches the surface, and by the time you are reading this, hundreds of great recordings will have been made and distributed by legendary figures and pianists who we aren't even aware of yet. The purpose here is to just offer a taste of this great music interpreted by pianists. These are listed in no particular order.

Red Garland
- *Red Alone, Volume 3*
- *Round about Midnight* (Miles Davis, leader)

Keith Jarrett
- *Live at the Blue Note*
- *Koln Concert*
- *Standards* (any of them)

Chick Corea
- *Return to Forever*
- *Now He Sings, Now He Sobs*

Erol Garner
- *Concert By the Sea*

Bill Evans
- *Portrait in Jazz*
- *Live at the Village Vanguard*
- *We Will Meet Again*

Joey Calderazzo
- *In the Door*
- *Tales from the Hudson* (Michael Brecker, leader)

Robert Glasper
- *So Beautiful*

Oscar Peterson
- *A Jazz Portrait of Frank Sinatra*

Brad Meldau
- *Live in Tokyo*

Benny Green
- *Testifyin'*
- *In This Direction*

Christian Sands
- *Reach*

Fred Hersch
- *Evanessence: A Tribute to Bill Evans*

Sullivan Fortner
- *The Window* (Cecile McLorin Salvant, leader)

Monty Alexander
- *Triple Treat*
- *Facets*

Cedar Walton
- *Firm Roots*

Jelly Roll Morton
- *Black Bottom Stomp*

Fats Waller
- *Honeysuckle Rose* (1934 version)

McCoy Tyner
- *A Love Supreme* (John Coltrane, leader)

Roger Kallaway
- *A Duet of One* (Eddie Daniels, leader)

Herbie Hancock
- *Maiden Voyage*
- *A New Standard*
- *Gershwin's World*

Aaron Parks
- *Bounce* (Terence Blanchard, leader)

Lenny Tristano
- *Line Up*

John Campbell
- *Live at Maybeck Recital Hall*

Kenny Barron
- *New York Attitude*

Kenny Werner
- *Introducing the Trio*

Tamir Hendelman
- *Playground*

Ahmad Jamal
- *At the Pershing*

Phineas Newborn
- *The Piano Artistry of Phineas Newborn, Jr.*

Hank Jones
- *The Great Jazz Trio*

Tommy Flanagan and Hank Jones
- *Ladybird*

Horace Silver
- *Hardbop Grandpop*

Wynton Kelly
- *Someday My Prince Will Come*

George Shearing
- *The Best of George Shearing*

Marian McPartland
- *Interview Program on NPR*

Dave Brubeck
- *Dave Brubeck's Greatest Hits*

Michel Petrucciani
- *Live at The Village Vanguard*

Mulgrew Miller
- *Dominion (Delpheayo Marsalis)*

Marcus Roberts
- *The Truth is Spoken Here*

Jacky Terrasson
- *Reach*

Bill Charlap
- *Bill Charlap Trio*

Harry Connick, Jr.
- *Newport Jazz Festival*
- *20*

Thelonious Monk
- *Monk Plays the Music of Duke Ellington*

Bud Powell
- *The Amazing Bud Powell, Vols. I & II*

Earl Hines
- *57 Varieties*

Jelly Roll Morton
- *Black Bottom Stomp*

Warren Bernhardt
- *Ain't Life Grand*

Marc Copland
- *Softly*

Barry Harris
- *Barry Harris at the Jazz Workshop*